Houghton
Mifflin
Harcourt

JOURNEYS
Close Reader

GRADE

4

Consumable

UNIT 1
Reaching Out

UNIT 2
Tell Me More

UNIT 3
Inside Nature

UNIT 4
Unbreakable Spirit

UNIT 5
Change It Up

UNIT 6
Paths to Discovery

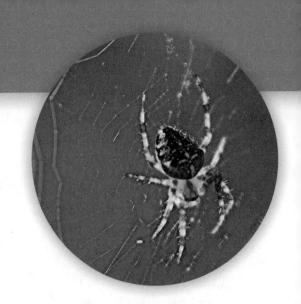

Houghton
Mifflin
Harcourt

JOURNEYS

Close Reader

UNIT 1
Reaching Out

Background If you were planning a children's center, what is one thing you would definitely want to have there? Lots of great books! However, if you did not have much money to spend, you would need to find another way to stock the library. In this text, you'll read about a young person's creative solution to this problem.

Setting a Purpose Read the text to learn how one boy helped others in his community.

Because of
BookEnds

Informational Text by John Korba

CLOSE READ
Notes

① Read As you read, collect and cite text evidence.
- Underline text that describes the problem faced by the Hollygrove organization.
- Circle Brandon's idea for solving the problem.

peculiar:

Think about what you're doing right now. You're learning something new. How are you doing it? You're reading a book.

You learn all kinds of things from books—things
5 that are fun, or important, or even **peculiar.** Books can make you smile and can comfort you when you're sad.

What if you didn't have this book, or any books? An eight-year-old boy named Brandon once thought
10 about that, and then he had a great idea.

A Little Boy's Big Idea

One day in 1998, Brandon Keefe was home from school
with a cold. His mother, Robin, had to go to a meeting, so
she took Brandon with her. The meeting was at a place
called Hollygrove in Los Angeles, California. Hollygrove is
15 a community organization for children and families.

At the meeting, Brandon played in a corner. The adults
were in a serious mood. They wanted to buy books for the
children's center, but they didn't have much money.
Brandon thought about this. He was positive he could use
20 his problem-solving talent to help.

The next day Brandon was back at school. His teacher
talked to the class about helping the community and asked
for ideas. Brandon told the class about the children's center
and its need for books. Then he **announced** his idea to hold
25 a giant book drive.

announced:

②**Reread** Reread lines 11–25. Summarize the events that led to Brandon's idea
to hold a book drive.

_____

_____

_____

_____

3 Read As you read, collect and cite text evidence.

- Underline text that describes the result of Brandon's first book drive.
- Circle the name of the organization Brandon's mother started.
- Underline details about the organization's work.

volunteers:

Brandon's class organized the book drive. Soon, donations of new and used books poured in. Teams of **volunteers,** which consisted of students, teachers, and administrators from the school, collected and sorted the
30 books. Meanwhile, Brandon did not mention this project to his mother.

Then one day Robin drove to school to pick up Brandon. He was waiting in the driveway with a great surprise: 847 books for the new library!
35 "That was one of the best days of my life," said Robin.

BookEnds Is Born

Robin knew there were many places that needed children's books. She saw that Brandon's idea could help them, too, so she started an organization called BookEnds.

BookEnds helps school kids set up book drives and get
40 the books to children who need them. Since 1998, BookEnds volunteers have donated more than a million books to more than three hundred thousand children.

Brandon is an adult now. He is still involved with BookEnds and intends to stay involved.

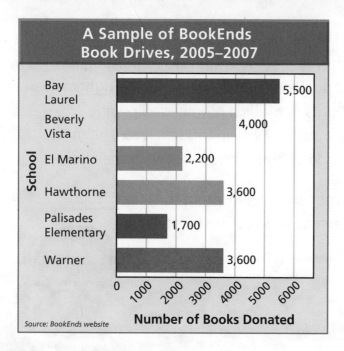

A Sample of BookEnds
Book Drives, 2005–2007

School	Number of Books Donated
Bay Laurel	5,500
Beverly Vista	4,000
El Marino	2,200
Hawthorne	3,600
Palisades Elementary	1,700
Warner	3,600

Source: BookEnds website

You Can Do It, Too!

45 Do you and your schoolmates have many books that you'll never read again? Then your school might want to hold a book drive.

Step 1: Find a place that needs books.

Step 2: Collect books that are still in good shape.

50 Step 3: Sort the books by reading level, so children don't get books that are too easy or too advanced.

Step 4: Deliver your books and watch the smiles appear!

---

④ Reread and Discuss Reread lines 45–52. Discuss how you might do a book drive at your school. How would you apply each step in the process?

SHORT RESPONSE

Cite Text Evidence   How does the graph on this page support ideas in the text? Cite details from the text in your response.

_____

_____

_____

Background Poet Langston Hughes (1902–1967) lived most of his life in a United States that did not legally grant him the same rights as white people. The U.S. Civil Rights Act, which promises all people equal rights, did not become law until 1964. In this text, you'll learn what Hughes urged people to do to bring about change in their lives.

Setting a Purpose Read the text to learn about the life of Langston Hughes and the message in one of his most famous poems.

Langston Hughes
A Poet and a Dreamer

Poetry

CLOSE READ
Notes

①ʀ Read As you read, collect and cite text evidence.

- Circle what Hughes believed about dreams.
- Underline text that tells why Hughes became interested in reading and writing.

inspired:

Langston Hughes was a famous African American poet whose words **inspired** and affected people all over the world. Like Dr. Martin Luther King Jr., Hughes believed that a
5   person's dream, or goal, could change the future. In his poem "Dreams," Hughes wrote about dreams and why they are so important.

As a child, Langston Hughes moved from city to city in the Midwest. Without a **permanent** home, he found

10 comfort in reading. Books were as nourishing to him as food. He grew into a strong reader and writer. He published his first poems and stories when he was in high school.

As a young man, Hughes traveled the world. He wrote about his encounters with all kinds of people. At home, he

15 had to deal with the unfair laws of segregation that kept people apart because of race. He thought deeply about injustice.

permanent:

2 Reread Reread lines 8–17. What events in Hughes's life may have prompted him to believe that a person's dream, or goal, could shape his or her future?

_____

_____

_____

_____

_____

_____

3 Read As you read, collect and cite text evidence.

- Underline text that describes Harlem.
- Circle what Hughes accomplished there.
- Underline what he captured in many of his works.

20 Hughes moved to Harlem, an African American neighborhood in New York City. Harlem became the place he preferred to all others. Here, writers, artists, and musicians were creating great works of art. Hughes's career as a writer blossomed. He went on to write numerous poems, stories, plays, and articles. Many of his works captured the culture and experiences of African
25 Americans, to be shared with readers around the world.

Langston Hughes is known as one of the most important poets of the twentieth century. His work has set an example for writers to come.

4 Reread Reread lines 18–25. Discuss how living in Harlem may have helped Hughes to become such a productive writer.

_____

_____

_____

_____

5 **Read** As you read, collect and cite text evidence.

- Circle the figurative language in the poem.
- Underline examples of repetition, or phrases that appear more than once.

Dreams

by Langston Hughes

Hold **fast** to dreams
For if dreams die
Life is a broken-winged bird
That cannot fly.

5   Hold fast to dreams
For when dreams go
Life is a **barren** field
Frozen with snow.

fast:

barren:

6 **Reread and Discuss** Reread lines 23–25. If "Dreams" captures "the culture and experiences of African Americans" during Hughes's lifetime, what can you infer about those experiences from the poem? Cite evidence from the text in your discussion.

SHORT RESPONSE

Cite Text Evidence What is the poet's message in "Dreams," and how does Hughes get it across? Cite text evidence from the poem in your response.

_____

_____

_____

_____

_____

© Houghton Mifflin Harcourt Publishing Company

Background Whether a book is eventually published on paper or on an electronic device, the procedure for turning an idea into a book is much the same. This text explains the procedure people follow and the jobs they do to create a book.

Setting a Purpose Read the text to learn how people turn ideas into books.

From Idea to Book

Informational Text by Kim Becker
illustrated by Remy Simard

CLOSE READ
Notes

① **Read** As you read, collect and cite text evidence.

- Underline any text that introduces a next step in the procedure.
- Circle words, such as *author,* that identify the roles people play in making a book.

product:

Have you ever wondered how a book is made? It takes a lot of people to make a book. It can take months, or even years, for a book to go from an idea to a finished **product.**

5   A book begins when an author comes up with an idea for a book. Authors get ideas in different ways. They may get ideas from their own lives, from watching the world around them, or from reading.

10   Next, an author may plan the book by making an **outline.** Sometimes authors do research to gather information. They may read books or articles. They may interview people or visit places.

15   Then, the author begins to write. Authors may write for months or years to finish a manuscript. A manuscript is the text an author produces for **publication.** Sometimes authors make many changes or even start over during the writing process.

20   Finally, the author sends the completed manuscript to a publisher. If the publisher decides to publish the book, the author works with an editor. An editor reads the manuscript. Then, he or she recommends changes to improve the

25   book. A copyeditor reads the manuscript to correct any grammatical errors.

②Reread Reread lines 20–25. Describe the roles performed by the publisher, editor, and copyeditor at this stage of the book creation procedure.

_____

_____

_____

_____

_____

③ Read As you read, collect and cite text evidence.

- Underline text that describes what a designer may do.
- Circle what the illustrator does after he or she knows where the pictures will appear in the book.

After an author makes the changes suggested by the copyeditor, a designer may decide how the book will look. The designer may choose the size, shape, and type styles for the book. Some picture book authors create
30 their own illustrations. If not, an illustrator is chosen to create pictures for the book.

First, the designer or illustrator decides what scenes to illustrate. He or she plans what pictures should go on
35 which pages. Next, the illustrator makes sketches of pictures that will go on each page. As they sketch, illustrators decide how the characters and setting will look. They use techniques such as **perspective** and point of view to clearly show story events.

40 The sketches are sent to the publishing company. The editor makes sure the pictures clearly tell the story. The designer checks how the words and pictures will fit together on the pages. He or she may make suggestions for improving the art.

perspective:

④ Reread Reread lines 27–44. Describe the differences in the designer's and illustrator's roles. Cite details from the text in your answer.

_____

_____

_____

_____

5 **Read** As you read, collect and cite text evidence.

- Underline the tools the illustrator may use and the kinds of changes he or she might make while working on the illustrations.
- Circle the sentence that tells what the designer does after receiving the finished art.

45   After the design changes are made, the illustrator begins creating the final pictures. The illustrator chooses what tools to use, such as paint, pastels, crayons, or a computer. As the illustrator

50   works, he or she may make many changes to the illustrations. The illustrator may change the colors, the perspective, or the **composition** of pictures. It may take months to create all the pictures.

composition:

The finished art is then sent to the publisher. The

55   designer adjusts how the pictures and words fit together on the pages. The completed pages are sent to the printer. Many books are still made into books with paper pages. However, many titles are available as eBooks, or electronic books.

6 **Reread** Reread lines 45–56. In what ways does the illustrator control or influence the overall appearance of the book? Cite evidence from the text in your answer.

_____

_____

_____

_____

7 **Read** As you read, collect and cite text evidence.

- Circle any words or phrases that are vague or confusing, or that you have questions about.
- Write in the margins any questions you wish the text had answered.

bindery:

60　　The printer uses huge printing presses to make the pages. Many pages of a picture book can be printed on one big sheet of paper. Printing presses can print thousands of pages in just a few hours. The big sheets of printed pages are then sent to the **bindery.** Here they are

65　folded into booklets called signatures. The signatures are gathered, along with the endpapers, and stitched together. The bound signatures are trimmed along the edges. Then, they are glued into the book cover. The finished books are

70　then sent to the publisher's warehouse. They are stored there until they are purchased by libraries and bookstores.

8 **Reread** Reread lines 60–72. What do you still want to know more about and why? Cite details from the text in your answer.

_____

_____

_____

_____

_____

9 Read As you read, collect and cite text evidence.

- Underline text that tells how the procedure for making eBooks differs from that for creating printed books.
- Circle the two sentences that explain where eBooks are stored and how customers get them.

E-readers

E-readers have changed how some books are made. Publishers sell some books as eBooks. However, some
75 authors do not use a publisher at all. Instead of sending a manuscript to a publisher, some authors turn their manuscripts into eBooks themselves. Many websites offer services that help authors **convert** their manuscripts into an e-reader format. Some websites offer the help of eBook
80 designers who make sure photos or illustrations match the words. Finally, an author's eBook is uploaded to virtual bookstores on the Internet. Customers can purchase and download eBooks from these websites.

convert:

10 Reread and Discuss Reread lines 73–83. Based on this information about e-readers, what do you think might happen to the procedure of making books in the future? Cite evidence from the text in your discussion.

SHORT RESPONSE

Cite Text Evidence What are some advantages and disadvantages to authors' creating eBooks themselves instead of working with a publisher to print their books? Cite text evidence in your response.

_____

_____

_____

_____

Background A fundraiser can be a great way to help your school or another organization you care about. It might sound like a lot of work (and it is), but with friends and adults on your team, you can do it—and at the same time make a difference in the world.

Setting a Purpose Read the text for step-by-step directions on how to plan a successful fundraiser.

The Secret to Super Fundraising

Informational Text

CLOSE READ
Notes

1 **Read** As you read, collect and cite text evidence.

- Underline text that describes what you need to decide first when you are thinking about raising money.
- Circle the first two steps you'll need to do before your fundraiser takes place.

Have you ever wanted to raise money for a school project or a good cause? First, you have to decide on the type of fundraising activity. Think about what you want to **accomplish.** Is your only goal

accomplish:

5 to raise money? If so, you might want to sell something, like candy bars or tickets to a raffle. The raffle prize could be anything from a store gift card to a gift basket.

10　Maybe your goal is to raise money and bring people in your school or community together. If so, hold a one-time event at a **specific** location. People in your neighborhood might appreciate a car wash or a bake sale. Or, your group could host a fun social event, such as a school dance. No matter what fundraiser you choose, following these ten

15　steps will lead you to success.

specific:

Before Your Fundraiser

Step 1: Get the okay! Explain your purpose to your group leaders, school officials, or parents. Make sure they are on board with your activity. Listen to their suggestions.

Step 2: Plan, plan, plan! Decide when and where your

20　fundraiser will take place. Check the calendar. Avoid conflicts with other events. Determine how many volunteers you will need, and list their tasks in a chart.

Jamal	Pick up donations for prizes.
Anna	Give tickets to sellers.
Maria	Keep track of ticket sales.

②Reread Reread lines 1–22. Summarize how you begin to think about and plan your fundraiser.

_____

_____

_____

_____

③ **Read** As you read, collect and cite text evidence.

- Circle the next steps you'll need to take.
- Underline the math equation for figuring out your total budget.

Step 3: Round up volunteers! Ask friends and family members to assist you. Have them tell everyone they know about your fundraiser. Ask them to contact businesses that might donate items.

budget:

Step 4: Go figure! Figure out a **budget**. How much money do you want to raise? How much will your fundraising activity cost? For example, if you have to buy

expense:

raffle prizes or items to sell, that is an **expense.** Any money you spend on making posters to advertise your fundraiser is another expense. Add together your expenses and the amount you want to raise. Use the total to help you figure out how much you need to sell and the price you need to charge.

Money to Raise	+	Expenses	=	Total Budget
$200	+	$0 (tickets and prizes were donated)	=	$200 (sell 100 tickets for $2 each)

Step 5: Spread the word! Use posters, fliers,

publicize:

websites, and social media to **publicize** your activity.

During Your Fundraiser

Step 6: Walk the talk! Encourage all volunteers to follow the plan. Be available to answer questions. Keep track of what you sell and spend.

Step 7: Bank it! Don't leave any money around. Give it to an adult for safekeeping.

After Your Fundraiser

Step 8: Count and account! As soon as possible, count
your money and pay your expenses. Let everyone know how
45   much money you raised, and inform them when and how it
will be donated or spent.

Step 9: Learn from experience! Review your activity
with your group. What went well? What went wrong? Make
notes to help you next time.

50   **Step 10: Mind your manners!** Be sure to thank
everyone who helped out.

Fun Is an Important Part of FUNdraising!

Fundraisers are hard work, but they can be fun, too! Think
about it. You spend time with your friends doing something
that is important to you. You make new friends. You learn
55   new skills and practice ones you already have. At the end,
you can feel really good about reaching your goal. Pat
yourself on the back for a job well done!

④ Reread and Discuss Reread lines 16–57. Discuss holding a fundraiser.
Which steps look challenging? Which steps look like they'd be easy? Tell why.

SHORT RESPONSE

Cite Text Evidence What are the key things to do before, during, and after your
fundraiser?

_____

_____

_____

_____

_____

Background Folktales are stories that have been passed orally from one storyteller to the next for generations. These stories are not necessarily true—or even based on true events—but they usually offer an explanation for something or teach a lesson. This play is based on a Japanese folktale about two brothers.

Setting a Purpose Read the text to discover what happens when two brothers trade jobs for a day.

Hoderi the Fisherman

Folktale retold by Kate McGovern

CLOSE READ
Notes

(1) Read As you read, collect and cite text evidence.

- Underline all the stage directions that appear in brackets and italic type.
- Circle the stage directions that you think are most important to the story.

Cast of Characters

Narrator

Hoderi (hoh DEH ree)

Hikohodemi (HIH koh hoh DEH mee)

Katsumi (kat SOO mee)

Sea King

Scene 1

[Setting: A small Japanese fishing village in the 1500s.]

Narrator: One day, two brothers—Hoderi, a hunter, and Hikohodemi, a fisherman—decide to trade jobs for a day.

Hoderi: Brother, let us make this day memorable by doing something special. I have always had a yearning to fish.

5 **Hikohodemi:** Good idea! But do not lose my fishing hook. With the shortage in iron, I cannot easily **replace** it.

Narrator: Alas, Hoderi is not a seafaring man. The first fish he catches swims away with the fishing hook.

Hoderi: *[To Hikohodemi]* I am afraid I lost your hook.

10 **Hikohodemi:** *[Looking horrified]* Hoderi! You betrayed my trust! By now the sea's **tidal shifts** have taken it far away.

Hoderi: *[Sorrowfully]* Then I shall search the entire sea until I find it. *[Hoderi dives into the water.]*

replace:

tidal shifts:

2 Reread Reread lines 5–13. What action takes place that you can only learn from the stage directions? Explain your answer.

_____

_____

_____

_____

_____

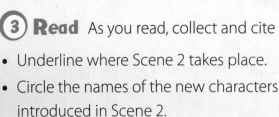

3 **Read** As you read, collect and cite text evidence.

- Underline where Scene 2 takes place.
- Circle the names of the new characters that are introduced in Scene 2.

Scene 2

[Setting: Underwater, near the Sea King's palace.]

    Narrator: Soon, Hoderi meets Katsumi, a Sea Princess.

15 **Katsumi:** Welcome! What brings you to our palace?

    Hoderi: Forgive me. I am looking for a lost fishing hook. It belongs to my brother.

    Katsumi: Perhaps my father, the Sea King, can help.

    Narrator: Hoderi tells the Sea King his story.

20 **Sea King:** The condition of the sea can make it dangerous, friend. We will help you search.

4 **Reread** Reread Scene 2. Where is Hoderi now? Who has entered the story, and how do these new characters help Hoderi?

_____

_____

_____

- Circle where and when Scene 3 takes place.
- Underline the text that tells what happens after Katsumi and Hoderi leave this setting.

CLOSE READ
Notes

Scene 3

[Setting: The Sea King's palace, weeks later.]

Narrator: Hoderi stayed in the palace. Soon, he and Katsumi fell in love. Then they received news.

Hoderi: *[Sadly]* The sea creatures have found the lost hook,
25   Katsumi. Now I must return home.

Katsumi: I will go with you, Hoderi.

Narrator: Katsumi hurries to tell her father.

Sea King: *[Upset]* You cannot leave! If you do, you will turn into a sea dragon! You will be an **outcast!**

outcast:

30   **Narrator:** Katsumi did not listen to her father. She traveled with Hoderi back to his village. But her father was right. One day, without warning, the Sea Princess became a dragon and disappeared into the foaming sea. Hoderi never saw her again.

6 **Reread and Discuss** Reread lines 30–34. If these events had taken place in a Scene 4, what would be the setting? Invent some dialogue for this scene.

SHORT RESPONSE

Cite Text Evidence   In how much detail are the play's settings described? Why might the author have described them this way?

_____

_____

_____

_____

UNIT 2
Tell Me More

Background Can you imagine gathering around the radio as a family to listen to shows the way some families gather to watch television shows today? Before television was invented, that's what people did. In this text you will learn about the history of radio as a source of both news and entertainment.

Setting a Purpose Read the text to discover how radio broadcasts first came to be and how they have changed over time.

The History of
RADIO

Informational Text by Vivian Fernandez

CLOSE READ
Notes

(1) Read As you read, collect and cite text evidence.

- Underline key events in the development and use of the radio.
- Circle all the headings that appear in the text.

The Beginning of Radio

We can't see them, but radio waves are all around us. In the late 1800s, Guglielmo Marconi used radio waves to send and receive a signal through the air. At first, the signal only went short

5 distances. Marconi kept working, and soon he was sending signals over several miles.

By the early 1900s, people were using radio technology to send and receive messages across

oceans. However, these messages were not voices. They had
10 to be sent in **Morse code.** Then, on December 24, 1906,
Reginald Fessenden made the first transmission of speech
and music. He had found a way to change the sounds of
voices and music into a signal that could be carried by radio
waves.

Radios in the Home

15 By the 1920s, more and more people had radios at home.
Families listened to the radio like we watch television. Many
listened to music, but soon radio stations came up with
different kinds of programs, which were often broadcast
live. Families could listen to the radio to hear music,
20 comedies, and stories. One show was maybe too exciting.
On October 30, 1938, Orson Welles presented "The War of
the Worlds." Millions of people listened to the radio show
about an alien attack, and some believed that what they
heard was real.

CLOSE READ
Notes

Morse code:

②**Reread** Reread lines 1–14. When did people start using radio technology to
send and receive messages across oceans? What did Reginald Fessenden do that
improved on early radio technology? Cite details from the text in your answer.

_____

_____

_____

_____

_____

③ **Read** As you read, collect and cite text evidence.

- Underline the sentences that explain what "soaps" were and why they got that name.
- Circle the forms of media that have created competition for radio broadcasting.

25   Another kind of radio drama told stories about families. They were called "soaps." This is because soap makers paid for most of these shows. Saturday mornings and after school were times for children's shows. *Buck Rogers in the Twenty-fifth Century*, *Superman*, and
30 *Popeye* were some children's shows.

    The radio was also a way for families to hear about news. On March 12, 1933, President Franklin D. Roosevelt gave the first of his "fireside chats." Later, during World War II, radio stations reported what was
35 happening.

    After World War II, people turned away from radio to television. Many radio programs stopped **airing.** Some shows that had been on the radio, such as *The Lone Ranger*, were now on television.

airing:

lone:

The Future of Radio

40 Today, radio has a lot of competition. Besides television and movies, many people turn to the Internet for entertainment and news. Internet radio does not use radio waves, but like radio, you can listen to music and shows anywhere. Regular radio is limited by how far
45 radio signals can reach. In time, we will see if radio survives this new kind of competition.

Early Days of Radio

1895　Guglielmo Marconi sends and receives first radio signal through the air

1901　Marconi receives first radio signal across the Atlantic Ocean

1906　Reginald Fessenden sends first transmission of human voice

1912　A message about the RMS *Titanic* sinking is sent through radio transmission, saving many lives

1920　First radio commercial broadcast in the United States reports results of presidential election

1921　First broadcast of baseball and football games

1922　First radio commercial in the United States (for **real estate** in New York)　　　**real estate:**

1926　First national network is formed: National Broadcasting Company (NBC)

④ Reread and Discuss　Reread lines 40–46. What advantage does the Internet have over radio, television, and movies shown in theaters? Cite evidence from the text in your discussion.

SHORT RESPONSE

Cite Text Evidence　Reread the timeline under "Early Days of Radio." Compare and contrast the information in the list with the information in the text. Which is more specific? Which is more complete? Cite text evidence in your response.

_____

_____

_____

_____

_____

_____

Background Although you may be familiar with the fact that moviemakers use special effects, you may not know what these effects are or how they work. In this text, you have the chance to learn about several of the techniques that filmmakers employ to create special effects.

Setting a Purpose Read the text to learn about specific techniques people use to create special effects in movies.

HOW
Do They Do
THAT?

Informational Text by Allan Giles

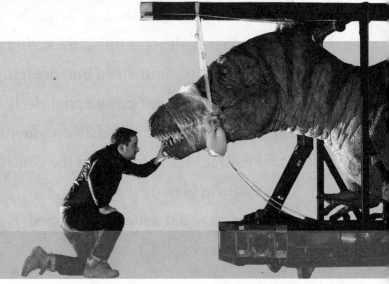

CLOSE READ
Notes

① Read As you read, collect and cite text evidence.

- Circle the sentence in the second paragraph that identifies the topic of this selection.
- Underline any subtopics mentioned in the text of that paragraph.

sequences:

Today's movies contain all sorts of make-believe characters and dangerous or seemingly impossible **sequences.** How do moviemakers create such characters and actions? How do they make them look believable? They use special effects.

There are many different kinds of special effects used in movies. Some examples include computer animation, blue-screen or green-screen filming, and model making. Others
10 are makeup effects, **stunt** effects, and sound effects. The whole movie industry changes as new special-effects techniques are developed. New techniques lead to more exciting possibilities!

The movie *Jurassic Park* won awards for special effects.
15 Director Steven Spielberg and his team of special-effects artists needed to make a variety of dinosaurs seem to come to life. They worked for three years to update old special-effects technologies and to develop new ones for the film.

Imagine you are a movie director. The movie calls for an
20 actress to hang from the side of a skyscraper. You don't want to risk the actress's life by asking her to dangle hundreds of feet in the air. So how do you film this in a way that looks realistic? You use a blue screen or green screen.

stunt:

(2) **Reread** Reread lines 1–13. What is the main topic of this selection, and what are some subtopics? Based on the first two paragraphs, what do you think is the author's purpose for writing this text?

_____

_____

_____

_____

_____

③ **Read** As you read, collect and cite text evidence.

- Underline sentences that introduce specific techniques or kinds of special effects.
- Circle the name of one technique used to create CGI effects.

To use the blue- or green-screening technique, filmmakers first film the background scene. In this case, they film the side of a skyscraper. Then, in the movie studio, they film the actress hanging from a rope in front of a blue or green screen. So now there are two pieces of film. One has the background scene of the skyscraper. One has the actress.

silhouette:

Then the special-effects department uses special filters to block out the green background to create a **silhouette** of the actress. This silhouette is then placed on the skyscraper background. Finally, they add the film of the actress in her silhouette.

Another movie special effect is Computer-Generated Imagery (or CGI). This technology has seen great advancements in the past twenty years. Some films, such as the *Shrek* movies, are entirely computer generated. Others, such as *Avatar,* combine computer-generated effects with live actors.

transformed:

One of the most popular CGI effects is the motion-capture technique used in *Avatar.* An actor wears special equipment with sensors placed at various points around the body. The actor's movements are captured, or copied, by special software. These movements are **transformed** into realistic computer **simulations.**

simulations:

32

The red lights on this special suit help the computer record what the actor does. The movements of the robot on the screen are exactly the same as the actor's movements.

All these special-effects technologies allow filmmakers to create movies that never could have been created before. Filmmakers can now produce an unlimited variety of characters, landscapes, and even virtual worlds through the use of special effects. As special-effects techniques continue to advance, so will the ability of movies to make the impossible seem possible.

④ Reread and Discuss Reread lines 36–47. Then review the photo and its caption. What does the photo add to the text? Is it necessary for understanding the text? Use details from the text, photo, and caption to support your opinion.

SHORT RESPONSE

Cite Text Evidence   What does the author conclude are the benefits of special-effects technologies? Cite one example from the text that supports this conclusion.

_____

_____

_____

_____

Background If you were going to create chalk drawings on the sidewalk, would you know how to make your colors as vivid and long-lasting as possible? Would you know how to blend them? This text reveals these secrets and may even inspire you to do some sidewalk art of your own.

Setting a Purpose Read the text to learn about sidewalk chalk art and the techniques artists use to make it interesting.

Sidewalk Artists

Readers' Theater by Sam Rabe

CLOSE READ
Notes

① **Read** As you read, collect and cite text evidence.

- Circle the text that shows which character speaks each line of dialogue.
- Underline text that describes the first few steps the characters take in making wet-chalk drawings.

Cast of Characters

Narrator

Ms. Lee

Kayla

Zack

Narrator: On a sunny day in southern Texas, Ms. Lee's students gathered in the school playground.

Ms. Lee: Tomorrow is the day of the sidewalk chalk-art festival. The principal has given us permission to practice

5 our wet-chalk drawing on the playground pavement, which will be our studio. Remember, whenever you want to draw on a sidewalk, always ask an adult in charge for permission before you draw. Now let's review the steps of wet-chalk drawing. What do we do first?

10 **Narrator:** As the students told her the steps in order, Ms. Lee wrote them on a large pad of paper. When she finished writing, she **yanked** the sheet off the pad and displayed the directions so everyone could read them. Then the students chose and soaked their pieces of chalk. Meanwhile, Kayla

15 and Zack planned their drawing.

Kayla: Let's draw a jungle feast. Parrots can be eating all kinds of fruit.

Zack: I'll draw a model train carrying food to the birds.

yanked:

---

2 Reread Reread lines 1–15. Based on the dialogue you have read so far, what might you expect to see as the first step on the list of directions for wet-chalk drawing? Cite evidence from the text to support your answer.

_____

_____

_____

_____

_____

3 Read As you read, collect and cite text evidence.

- Circle the punctuation marks that tell you which sentences to exclaim and which to say as a question.
- Underline the simile the narrator uses.

curve:

Narrator: The students removed their pieces of chalk
20 from the water and drew. As Zack drew a sweeping
curve of train track, his hand knocked over the jar of
water. He and Kayla watched water streak across their
drawing.

Zack: Our drawing is ruined!

25 **Kayla:** Don't be so concerned! Quick, blend the water
and the chalk together! Now let's layer on more chalk
and smear it around.

Narrator: Kayla and Zack worked quickly. The smeared
colors looked glorious, like rich, thick frosting on a cake.

30 **Ms. Lee:** That looks great! That's a neat technique you're
using, kids. Are you two interested in taking part in the
chalk-art festival tomorrow? The schedule for the festival
says that drawing starts at 9:00 a.m.

Kayla and Zack: Sure!

35 **Kayla:** Tomorrow we'll spill water on our drawing
on purpose.

Zack: Then we'll know just what to do!

4 Reread Reread lines 24–37. How would you describe the mood or feeling in this section of the readers' theater? Cite the text evidence that supports your conclusion.

_____

_____

_____

⑤ Read As you read, collect and cite text evidence.

- Circle the text feature that the author uses to show the order of the steps in the directions.
- Write any questions you have that would help clarify the directions.

Making Wet Chalk Drawings

1. Choose your pieces of chalk, and put them in a jar.
2. Fill the jar with water to cover three quarters of the length of the chalk. Let the chalk soak for a few minutes, but don't let it **dissolve.**
3. Remove the wet chalk from the jar.
4. Draw!
5. Let your drawing dry.

dissolve:

⑥ Reread and Discuss Reread the directions for making wet-chalk drawings. Do you think the order of the steps matters? Why? What would happen if you changed the order of certain steps? Cite details from the text in your discussion.

SHORT RESPONSE

Cite Text Evidence What additional step or information might you add to the directions? Give a reason for each addition you suggest and support it with evidence from the text.

_____

_____

_____

_____

_____

Background A field guide is a reference book people use to learn about the natural world. Field guides usually have short entries that use words and pictures to describe the features of various plants and animals. This selection includes a few entries about snakes of the Southwest.

Setting a Purpose Read the text to learn about snakes, including a few snakes that live in the southwestern part of the United States.

FIELD GUIDE to
Snakes of the
Southwest

Informational Text by Patrick Sutter

CLOSE READ
Notes

(1) **Read** As you read, collect and cite text evidence.
- Underline text that describes what snakes can do.
- Circle text that tells how people feel about snakes.

ecosystem:

Snakes are amazing. They have no arms or legs, but they move quickly. They have no ears, but heat-sensing organs help them find their prey. Snakes survive in almost every **ecosystem** on
5 Earth.

Many people fear snakes. Some individuals have even
fainted at the sight of these reptiles, but this is no one's fault.
It's true that some snakes are dangerous. Yet many are not.
In fact, most snakes help local farmers by eating pests.

10 People imagine a snake's skin is slimy, but it is made of dry
scales.

This reference guide gives information about three
snakes from the Southwest.

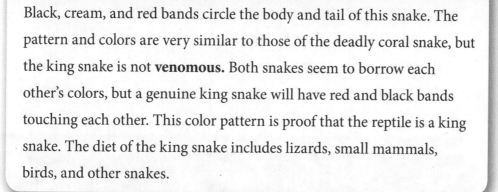

Common name: Mountain King Snake
Scientific name: Lampropeltis zonata
Size: 20–40 inches
Habitat: mountains, damp woods
Nonvenomous

Black, cream, and red bands circle the body and tail of this snake. The
pattern and colors are very similar to those of the deadly coral snake, but
the king snake is not **venomous.** Both snakes seem to borrow each
other's colors, but a genuine king snake will have red and black bands
touching each other. This color pattern is proof that the reptile is a king
snake. The diet of the king snake includes lizards, small mammals,
birds, and other snakes.

habitat:

venomous:

②Reread Reread pages 38 and 39. Describe a few things snakes can do, as well
as how some people feel about them.

_____

_____

_____

_____

© Houghton Mifflin Harcourt Publishing Company • Image Credits: ©Suzanne L. Collins/Photo Researchers, Inc.

③ **Read** As you read, collect and cite text evidence.

- Underline text that describes what snakes look like.
- Circle text that tells how snakes behave.
- In the chart, circle pairs of traits that go together.

Common name: Western Diamond-Backed
     Rattlesnake
Scientific name: Crotalus atrox
Size: 30–90 inches
Habitat: dry areas, such as deserts and
     rocky foothills
Venomous

This is the largest snake in the West. It eats small mammals, birds, and reptiles. People fear this snake because it is very dangerous. Even a dead rattlesnake can bite! Its jaws can still open when touched and can still inject venom. Scientists do not apologize for trying to protect rattlesnakes, though. They have insisted that in spite of the danger, rattlesnakes are important. This snake will not attack, but it will defend itself. First, it shakes its tail to make a rattling sound. This is a signal to back off!

Common names: Desert Threadsnake or
     Western Blind Snake
Scientific name: Leptotyphlops humilis
Size: 6–13 inches
Habitat: mountain slopes, deserts,
     rocky foothills
Nonvenomous

This tiny, harmless snake can be brown, purple, or pink in color. One of its two common names refers to its thin, wormlike body. The other refers to its lack of eyes. Instead of eyes that see, this snake has two black spots on its face. The threadsnake **burrows** for its food under plant roots and rocks and in ant nests. It eats ants and other small insects.

burrows:

Traits of Southwestern Snakes

TRAITS	MOUNTAIN KING SNAKE	DIAMOND-BACKED RATTLESNAKE	DESERT THREADSNAKE
venomous		🐍	
nonvenomous	🐍		🐍
desert habitat		🐍	🐍
mountain habitat	🐍		🐍
large size	🐍	🐍	
small size			🐍

traits:

④ Reread and Discuss   Study the chart on this page. Is there a snake that has both of the traits in a pair? How is that possible?

SHORT RESPONSE

Cite Text Evidence   How do some people view snakes? What evidence contrasts with those views? Cite evidence in your response.

_____

_____

_____

_____

_____

Background Your favorite song has rhythm, but your speech has rhythm, too. Rhythm is a pattern of beats. It makes speech, and poetry, sound better and draws attention to certain words and ideas. In "The Song of the Night," the poet uses rhyme and repetition, or repeating certain words and phrases, to create rhythm.

Setting a Purpose Read the poem to discover how the poet uses rhyme and repetition to create rhythm.

Dance to the Beat

Poetry, with an Introduction by Adam Fogelberg

CLOSE READ
Notes

1 **Read** As you read, collect and cite text evidence.
- Underline phrases that are repeated in the poem.
- Circle words that rhyme.

Dancers move their bodies to the beat, or
rhythm, of music. Poems are like music and
dance: They, too, have rhythm. As you read the
following poem about dancing, listen for its
5   rhythm.

The Song of the Night
by Leslie D. Perkins

I dance to the tune
of the stars and the moon.
I dance to the song of the night.

I dance to the **strains**
5   of a cricket's **refrain.**
I dance to the fireflies' light.

I dance to the breeze
and the whispering trees.
I dance to the meteor's flight.

10   I dance to the beat
of the summertime heat.
I dance to the **pulse** of the night.

strains:

refrain:

pulse:

---

②Reread and Discuss Reread the poem. Discuss what the poet is saying about the night. How might the breeze and whispering trees have rhythm? What about the fireflies' light? Cite evidence from the text in your discussion.

SHORT RESPONSE

Cite Text Evidence   How do rhyme and repetition connect lines and stanzas within the poem? Cite details from the text in your response.

_____

_____

_____

_____

_____

UNIT 3
Inside Nature

Background Hurricanes are storms with incredibly powerful winds and heavy rain, and they can cause more damage than any other kind of storm on the planet. In 2005, Hurricane Katrina landed at the Gulf Coast. This text, a newspaper article, was written a year after the storm.

Setting a Purpose Read the text to learn about the damage done by Hurricane Katrina and the recovery efforts undertaken in the first year after the storm.

Recovering from Katrina

Informational Text by Alice Young

CLOSE READ
Notes

① **Read** As you read, collect and cite text evidence.

- Underline text that tells about the paths of Hurricanes Andrew and Katrina.
- Circle facts about the damage each storm caused.

Life has changed along the Gulf Coast in the past year. One year ago, Hurricane Katrina was churning in the warm, moist air of the Gulf of Mexico as a Category 5 storm. This is the

5 strongest and most destructive rating for a hurricane. All along the Gulf Coast, residents were bracing for the impact of this mighty storm.

On the morning of August 29, Hurricane Katrina made
landfall in southern Louisiana. She was now a Category 3

10 hurricane with winds near 125 miles per hour. She left
behind a path of destruction in Louisiana, Mississippi, and
Alabama. Damages in New Orleans and along the Gulf
Coast totaled $108 billion. This made Katrina the costliest
and most destructive natural disaster in U.S. history. Most

15 Atlantic hurricanes move north as they approach the
Atlantic coast of the United States and do not land. Some
storms hit Florida, and a few move into the Gulf of Mexico
as Katrina did.

Before Katrina, Hurricane Andrew had been the

20 costliest storm in U.S. history. Hurricane Andrew hit
southern Florida on August 24, 1992, as a Category 5 storm.
Violent winds and storm **surges** destroyed many homes and
businesses.

Nearly 250,000 people were left homeless. Hurricane

25 Andrew moved across Florida. Then it moved into the Gulf
of Mexico. It struck south-central Louisiana as a Category 3
storm on August 26, 1992.

CLOSE READ
Notes

surges:

2 Reread Reread lines 1–27. Compare Katrina and Andrew regarding the path
each took and the damage each caused.

_____

_____

_____

_____

_____

(3) Read As you read, collect and cite text evidence.

- Underline text that tells why water becomes such a menace in hurricanes.
- Underline the reason most of New Orleans flooded.
- Circle text that tells what aid agencies did to help.

levees:

A hurricane pulls up a dome of seawater that travels with the hurricane. The high water dome creates the 30 storm surge. Strong winds create giant waves. The storm surge often causes the greatest damage in a hurricane.

Flooding caused much of the damage from Hurricane Katrina. **Levees** that separate New Orleans from surrounding lakes broke. These breaks caused 35 most of New Orleans to lie under floodwater. Some parts of the city were covered by twenty feet of water. Huge twenty- to thirty-foot storm surges from Katrina also caused massive flooding in coastal cities of Mississippi and Alabama.

40 After Hurricane Katrina, hundreds of thousands of people were left homeless. They had to find temporary housing in hotels, homes of friends or family, or in shelters. Thousands of shelters were set up in schools, community centers, and various other buildings.

45 The Red Cross, government agencies, and other relief groups set up the shelters. One large shelter was set up at the Astrodome in Houston, Texas. In early September 2005, it housed more than 11,000 hurricane victims.

A year after Hurricane Katrina, many homes and 50 other buildings still need repair. About one third of New Orleans's schools, hospitals, and libraries are still closed. Thousands of people whose homes were destroyed continue to live in trailers provided by FEMA, the Federal Emergency Management Agency. Relief

55 agencies, such as FEMA and the Red Cross, continue to help rebuild damaged homes. They continue to **relocate** people whose homes were destroyed.

Recovering from such widespread destruction has been a huge task. Some people have been able to repair or rebuild
60 their homes and businesses during the past year. Many residents have chosen to remain in the region where they grew up. They are determined to rebuild their homes, their communities, and their lives.

The volunteer response to Hurricane Katrina has been
65 the largest in U.S. history. Hundreds of thousands of people across the country have stepped in to help in any way they can. Some come to the Gulf Coast region and volunteer for a weekend. Others stay for months at a time to help in the rebuilding effort. Much has been accomplished in the past
70 year to rebuild the Gulf Coast. Yet much remains to be done.

CLOSE READ
Notes

relocate:

(4) Reread and Discuss What could have been done to make sure New Orleans would be safe? Cite details from the text in your discussion.

SHORT RESPONSE

Cite Text Evidence Reread lines 40–71. Summarize the response of aid agencies and volunteers to Hurricane Katrina. Why do you think so many people wanted to help?

_____

_____

_____

_____

_____

Background Twisters are tornadoes: powerful storms that can cause lots of damage when they plow through areas where people live. They are called twisters because the funnel of wind appears to be twisting, or rotating.

Setting a Purpose Read the text to learn where tornadoes happen, how they form, and how you can protect yourself from them.

Twisters

Informational Text by Laura Dameron

CLOSE READ
Notes

① Read As you read, collect and cite text evidence.

- Underline text that tells why Texas has the most tornadoes in the United States.
- Circle text that explains how tornadoes form.

tornado:

On March 28, 2000, a **tornado** passed through downtown Fort Worth, Texas. In about ten minutes, the tornado's crushing force left the city littered with debris. Right behind it, a second
5   tornado damaged buildings in nearby towns. Each fallen slab added to the wreckage and rubble.

Around one thousand tornadoes form in the United
States every year. Of all the states, Texas has the most
10 tornadoes. It has an average of 153 twisters each year. Texas
is an **ideal** setting for tornadoes. This is because it is located
between the warm air of the Gulf of Mexico and the cool air
of the Rocky Mountains.

Supercells and Funnel Clouds

Tornadoes form when warm air moving in different
15 directions rises and cools. If the air keeps rising and
spinning, it can develop into a thunderstorm called a
supercell. It can then turn into a tornado.

Meteorologists, scientists who study the weather, can't
predict exactly when a tornado will strike. But, they can use
20 radar to track storms. When a supercell grows stronger, the
radar measures its **rotation** for changes in speed.
Meteorologists can also spot tornadoes by studying jet
streams. They do this by looking at computer models and
satellite pictures for signs of thunderstorms.

ideal:

rotation:

②Reread Reread lines 8–17. Explain how tornadoes form and why Texas is
such a good location for tornadoes.

_____

_____

_____

_____

③ **Read** As you read, collect and cite text evidence.

- Underline text that explains what warm air and cool air do when a tornado is forming.
- Circle details of what you should do if you hear a tornado warning.

Birth of a Tornado

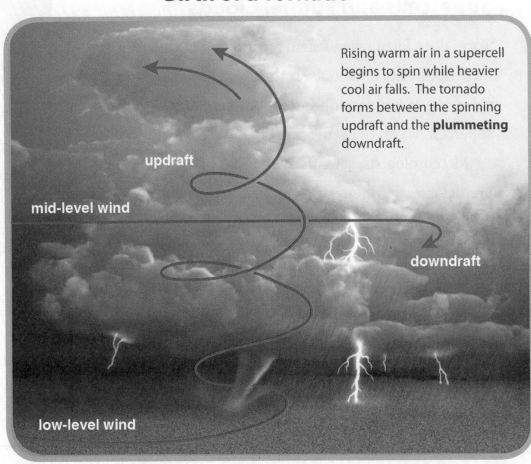

Rising warm air in a supercell begins to spin while heavier cool air falls. The tornado forms between the spinning updraft and the **plummeting** downdraft.

updraft

mid-level wind

downdraft

low-level wind

plummeting:

Tornado Safety

25   Buildings in tornado zones need to be constructed with strong roofs and **foundations**. Weaker buildings made from timbers can be made stronger with steel and concrete. Weather reports are used to alert residents that a tornado

30   is on its way. Tornado sirens, used in several states, also warn people.

foundations:

A tornado watch is announced when conditions are right for a tornado. A tornado warning means that a tornado has been seen. If you hear a tornado warning,

35 don't stay outside and don't try to save your favorite possessions. Flying debris can injure people and damage buildings, from tenements to skyscrapers. Follow these simple rules:

• Get inside a sturdy building.

40 • Move to an inside room.

• Stay away from windows. If the glass trembles, it may break.

• Wait until the storm has passed before going outdoors.

④ Reread and Discuss Reread lines 32–44. Discuss what you should do in case of a tornado. What do you think is the reason for each rule?

SHORT RESPONSE

Cite Text Evidence Explain how the "Birth of a Tornado" diagram supports the information in the text. Cite specific details in your response.

_____

_____

_____

_____

_____

Background Thousands of miles to the south of the United States lies Antarctica, a frozen continent at the southernmost spot on Earth. No one had ever seen Antarctica until about 200 years ago, and it wasn't until the mid-1960s that a permanent research station was built there.

Setting a Purpose Read the text to learn about Antarctica and what scientists are studying there.

Cold, Cold Science

Informational Text by Dewey Badeaux

CLOSE READ
Notes

1 Read As you read, collect and cite text evidence.

- Underline text that describes what Antarctica is made up of.
- Circle the detail that tells the purpose of the Palmer Station.

environment:

At Palmer Station in Antarctica, scientists live and work in a world of ice. A giant ice sheet that covers the continent helps scientists at Palmer Station understand an **environment** that doesn't
5 exist anywhere else on Earth.

Home Away from Home

Palmer Station is one of three bases in Antarctica operated by the United States. It is located on Anvers Island, just west of the Antarctic Peninsula in the northwestern part of the continent. Scientists at Palmer Station live at the base year-round and perform field studies in the surrounding environment. One visiting writer, Kate Madin, said, "This town has a single purpose, and everyone here is a part of it: scientific research on the Antarctic coastal ecosystem."

Frozen Sculptures

The **unique** features of the Antarctic landscape give the scientists at Palmer Station many frozen clues to use in their research. Antarctica is glacier country. A glacier is a **mass** of ice and snow formed on land over thousands of years. A glacier slowly moves across land due to gravity and its great weight. The Antarctic ice sheet, an enormous glacier, covers 98 percent of the continent and contains approximately 5 million square miles of ice, averaging 7,000 feet thick. The Antarctic ice sheet is the largest single mass of ice on Earth, and it contains about 70 percent of Earth's freshwater.

10

15

20

unique:

mass:

2 Reread Reread "Home Away from Home" and "Frozen Sculptures." Summarize what each section is about.

_____

_____

_____

_____

_____

③ **Read** As you read, collect and cite text evidence.

- Underline what the scientists at Palmer Station study.
- Circle text that describes how windy, cold, and dry Antarctica is.

25   Nearly half of Antarctica's coastline is made up of thick, floating ice called ice shelves. Ice shelves result from the Antarctic ice sheet's movement towards the coastline. They form where the ice sheet meets the water. Palmer Station is located near the Larsen Ice Shelf.

frigid:

    Icebergs can be seen in the **frigid** waters near
30 Antarctica's coast. An iceberg is a large mass of floating ice broken off from a glacier or ice shelf. Icebergs can be the size of an automobile or a small country! An iceberg's movement is influenced by ocean currents and winds. Eventually, icebergs melt and disappear.

35   Scientists at Palmer Station study how the Antarctic ice sheet moves and how the temperature of the ocean changes over time. They learn how changes to the ice sheet and ice shelves affect animals that live in Antarctica. The scientists' work also helps them
40 understand how changes in Earth's climate can impact the rest of the world.

Scientists at Palmer Station believe that many icebergs came from the Wilkins Ice Shelf when it broke apart in 2008.

Windiest, Driest, Coldest

Antarctica is a place of climate **extremes.** Did you know
that it is the windiest place on Earth? During a blizzard, the
wind in Antarctica is so strong that it can change the shape

45 of ice and rocks. The strongest winds are found along the
coast of the continent and on the Antarctic Peninsula.

Antarctica may not be hot, but much of the continent is
the driest place on Earth. It is a desert! Because the air is so
cold and dry, it is hard for clouds to form and make rain or

50 snow in the central part of the continent. Not only is
Antarctica the world's driest desert, it's also the largest!

The temperature in Antarctica's interior during the
winter can get as cold as –94° F. However, in summer, the
temperature along the Antarctic Peninsula can climb to

55 almost 60° F. Because the conditions in Antarctica can be so
harsh, scientists are very busy there during the warmer
summer season. During certain weeks in summer, the sun
does not set at all—there is daylight 24 hours a day! The
warm temperatures cause the ice along the coast to melt

60 and can impact Antarctica's wildlife.

4 Reread Reread lines 24–41. Explain what the Palmer Station scientists study
and what it helps them learn.

_____

_____

_____

_____

5 Read As you read, collect and cite text evidence.

- Circle the kinds of wildlife found around Antarctica.
- Underline details about what scientists measure to judge their effect on penguins.

Antarctica's Wildlife

Zoologists are scientists who study wildlife, from very small to very large. At Palmer Station, scientists measure temperatures on the coast and in the ocean. They also get information from satellites that orbit the earth. This

65 information helps zoologists learn how changes in climate affect the krill, seabirds, and other animals that make up Antarctica's ecosystem.

Krill live in the seas surrounding Antarctica. Similar to shrimp in size and structure, an **individual** Antarctic

70 krill is about 2 inches long. Krill is an important source of food for much larger fish, birds, and **mammals.** Thousands of krill swim together in swarms, making it easy for whales, seals, and penguins to catch them.

Dragonfish, cod, and icefish live in the Southern

75 Ocean, which surrounds Antarctica. These fish species mainly live at the bottom of the ocean and feed on krill and other creatures. Starfish, squid, and sea spiders live in the Southern Ocean as well.

Seals can be found relaxing in the cold waters of

80 Antarctica. Of the many different types of seals in Antarctica, the elephant seal is the largest. A male elephant seal can weigh up to 8,000 lbs. Many scientists believe that seals are most similar to otters and skunks. On the other hand, other scientists believe seals are more

85 closely related to bears!

Seals are able to hold their breath for a long time while swimming underwater. Some seals can swim up to 50

individual:

mammals:

miles a day when they are hunting for krill, fish, and penguins.

Enormous whales live in the Southern Ocean, too. Like
90 other mammals, whales need air to live. Most mammals,
such as seals, breathe through their noses and mouths.
Whales, however, breathe through an opening on the top of
their heads. Humpbacks, orcas, and many other types of
whales can be seen in the icy seas of Antarctica.

95 Different kinds of seabirds call Antarctica home. They
live and nest on Antarctica's shores and look for food in the
water. The albatross is one kind of seabird that lives in
Antarctica. It has a wingspan of 11 feet, making it the
largest flying bird in the world.

100 Penguins, another kind of seabird, live and nest in large
groups. Unlike other seabirds, these black and white birds
cannot fly. Penguins walk on land and swim in the
Southern Ocean to look for food.

At Palmer Station, scientists are very interested in
105 penguins. These scientists study how the sun, **atmosphere,**   **atmosphere:**
ocean, and food supply cause the penguin population to rise
or fall. Because Antarctica is so **isolated,** scientists can
focus on a single species and learn a lot about how that   **isolated:**
species survives.

Elephant seal

6 Reread and Discuss Reread lines 100–109. Why do scientists have a
particular interest in penguins? Cite text evidence in your discussion.

(7) Read As you read, collect and cite text evidence.

- Underline text that describes what Antarctica might have been like long ago.
- Circle text that describes the problem scientists have found.

Looking Back and to the Future

fossils:

110 **Fossils** discovered on the islands near the Antarctic Peninsula have led many scientists to believe that Antarctica was once a much warmer place, where small, bird-like dinosaurs roamed the land. Fossils of ancient trees also suggest it was warm enough for flowers to

115 bloom. Can you imagine Antarctica warm and sunny?

Scientists take an ice sample for their research.

Too much sun, of course, is a problem. Scientists have discovered a hole in the ozone layer in the atmosphere above Antarctica. The ozone layer is a **gaseous** shield that protects us from the sun's powerful rays. Without this

120 protection, most life on Earth could not survive. To help shrink the ozone hole, governments in many countries are teaming up to decrease pollution. In time, scientists believe this will help solve the problem.

The work that scientists do at Palmer Station allows

125 people around the world to learn about our planet's climate, oceans, and animal life. By studying clues from the past and what is happening today, they also uncover information that helps us make important predictions about the future.

gaseous:

⑧ Reread and Discuss Reread lines 116–128. What might happen to Antarctica if we aren't able to shrink the ozone hole? What might that mean for the rest of the world? Cite evidence from the text in your discussion.

SHORT RESPONSE

Cite Text Evidence   What makes Antarctica such a unique place? Why is it worth studying? Cite details from the text in your response.

_____

_____

_____

_____

_____

_____

Background The following fable is from a collection that is over two thousand years old. These stories were said to have been written by a man named Aesop, although some people now believe that Aesop never really existed. The purpose of a fable is not only to tell a good story but also to teach a lesson.

Setting a Purpose Read the text to learn a lesson about what happens when individuals help one another.

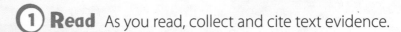

The Dove and the Ant

Fable retold by Anne O'Brien

① **Read** As you read, collect and cite text evidence.

- Underline text that describes what the Ant is doing.
- Circle the details that tell how the Dove helps the Ant.

fable:

This retelling of an old fable is set on the island of Puerto Rico, where a wide river, the Rio de la Plata, flows from the mountains down to the sea. Near the river stands a large ausubo tree.

5 A Dove sat in the branches of the ausubo tree. He was a social creature who liked to meet other animals.

At the base of the tree was an anthill. There an Ant was working to transport food for storage. The Dove watched her reinforce the anthill and clear the central chamber. He

10 saw her moving obstacles from the tunnels.

"What a hard worker!" remarked the Dove.

Not long after, he heard the Ant say in a tiny voice, "I'm so thirsty!"

The Dove wanted to help. He flew down to a lower

15 branch. "The river is not far," he called out to the Ant. "It is just beyond that tall grass."

At the riverbank, the Ant had a long drink. Then suddenly a gust of wind blew her into the water.

"Help!" cried the Ant. Hearing the Ant's cry, the Dove

20 grabbed a twig in his beak and dropped it into the water.

"Climb on and save yourself!" the Dove called. **Clinging**   clinging:

to the twig, the Ant was soon washed to shore.

② **Reread** Reread lines 5–22. What text details tell you whether the Dove is a helpful creature or not?

_____

_____

_____

_____

_____

3 **Read** As you read, collect and cite text evidence.

- Underline text that explains why the Dove helped the Ant.
- Circle details that show what the Ant thinks when she sees the hunter.

pleasure:

"How can I ever thank you?" the Ant asked the Dove. "Life is hard and such kindness is scarce."

25 "It was my **pleasure**," the Dove replied. "I like to help my fellow creatures. There can never be excess kindness in this world."

Thinking over the Dove's words, the Ant returned to work.

30 Later that day, a hunter named Rafael appeared, carrying a large sack. He spotted the Dove in the ausubo tree. He set to work near the anthill, building a bird trap.

The Ant saw the sack and the trap. "When the hunter catches a bird, he transfers it into the sack and carries it

35 away," the Ant thought.

Just then the Ant saw the Dove flying toward the trap. "Oh, no," said the Ant. "The Dove will be caught! I have to act quickly."

4 **Reread** Reread lines 23–38. What does the Ant decide to do when the hunter appears? Why does she decide that?

_____

_____

_____

⑤ Read As you read, collect and cite text evidence.

- Underline text that describes what the Ant does.
- Circle the dialogue that shows the Dove is safe.
- Put a check mark next to the story's lesson.

In a flash, the Ant crawled up Rafael's foot and bit his

40 ankle. The hunter cried out in pain. **Startled,** the Dove
flew higher up into the tree.

startled:

Rafael rubbed his ankle. "Too bad," he thought. "Now
I will have to catch my dinner elsewhere."

When the hunter had gone, the Dove turned to his

45 friend. "Now it is my turn to thank you," he said.

"It was my pleasure," the Ant replied.

*The lesson of the tale is this: The best way to make
friends is by exchanges of kind deeds.*

⑥ Reread and Discuss Reread lines 39–48. Do you agree that exchanging
kind deeds is the best way to make friends? Cite details from the text in your
discussion.

SHORT RESPONSE

Cite Text Evidence How does this story illustrate the lesson at the end? Does it do a
good job? Cite evidence from the text to support your opinion.

_____

_____

_____

_____

_____

Background The first of these two short poems about weather is a haiku, a form of poetry that started in Japan. The poet who wrote this haiku lived about 300 years ago. Haiku is made up of three lines. The first and third lines have five syllables, or beats, and the second line has seven.

Setting a Purpose Read these poems to see how much a poet can say about the weather with just a few words.

Wonderful Weather

Poetry

CLOSE READ
Notes

① **Read** As you read, collect and cite text evidence.

- Circle words for things you might wear or use outdoors when it's raining.
- Underline what keeps the rain out of a building.
- Circle the words in the second poem that rhyme.

sensory:

vivid:

Weather creates all kinds of **sensory** experiences. In other words, it's the perfect topic for a poem! What do you see, hear, and feel on a hot summer day? How about during a blizzard? The following
5 poems create **vivid** images of rainy weather and how people respond to it.

Spring Rain
by Buson

In the rains of spring,
An umbrella and raincoat
Pass by, **conversing**.

conversing:

Umbrella
by Rob Hale

Out there — wet
In here — dry
Cozy little roof
Between me and the sky

---

②Reread and Discuss Reread "Spring Rain." Discuss what the umbrella and the raincoat represent. Why does the poet say they are "conversing"?

SHORT RESPONSE

Cite Text Evidence Reread the two poems. Which poet do you think likes being outside? Which prefers to be inside? Cite details to support your ideas.

_____

_____

_____

_____

_____

UNIT 4
Unbreakable Spirit

Background In the mid-1800s, people began refining "rock oil," or petroleum, to make fuels and other products. The first modern oil well in the United States was drilled in Pennsylvania in 1859. This text, from an online encyclopedia entry, gives factual information about the beginnings of the oil industry in Texas.

Setting a Purpose Read the text to learn how the Texas oil industry began.

Spindletop

Informational Text

CLOSE READ
Notes

① Read As you read, collect and cite text evidence.

- Underline problems faced by the men who wanted to start the Texas oil industry.
- Circle the solution to each problem.

In the 1890s Texas produced only small amounts of oil. But one risk-taker thought that east Texas was worthy of further study. In 1892, Pattillo (puh TIH loh) Higgins, a self-taught **geologist**, began drilling for oil.

geologist:

5   He drilled near Beaumont, Texas, in an area called Spindletop Hill. Spindletop was a salt dome, a hill formed by rising underground mineral salts. Higgins's

first drills found nothing. His **financial** situation was
looking bad. So he hired Captain Anthony F. Lucas to take

10   over.

financial:

The Lucas Geyser

Lucas was a leading geologist with a reputation as an expert
on salt domes. He began drilling at Spindletop in 1899.
At first, he, too, had no luck. The money he relied on was
running out. Lucas escorted businessmen to Beaumont,

15   hoping that they would **invest** in the well. Most of them felt
that he did not deserve their help. But Lucas defended his ideas
about salt domes and oil. Finally, his investors were satisfied
that his project was worthwhile, and the funds came in.

   On the morning of January 10, 1901, Lucas's team drilled

20   down 1,139 feet—and found oil. "The Lucas Geyser," as it
came to be called, blew oil more than 150 feet in the air. In
time, it would produce 100,000 barrels per day. Until then, few
oil fields in Texas had produced more than 25 barrels per day!

invest:

②Reread Reread lines 1–23. How did Higgins and Lucas overcome problems
to start the oil industry in Texas? Cite details in your response.

_____

_____

_____

_____

_____

③ Read As you read, collect and cite text evidence.

- Underline text that tells how Spindletop affected the community.
- Circle words and phrases that describe growth.

Birth of an Industry

Spindletop was the largest oil well the world had ever
25   seen. By September 1901, six more wells were
producing oil in the area. Nearby Beaumont became
one of the first oil-fueled **boomtowns**. Workers,
merchants, and speculators rushed to the city. Its
population of 10,000 tripled in three months, and soon
30   it swelled to 50,000.

    The price of land skyrocketed along with the
population. One parcel that had been priced at $150
before the geyser sold for $20,000—and the buyer
resold it that same day for $50,000. In 1901 alone,
35   people invested about $235 million in Texas oil
production. Some became rich; others lost their money.

    Spindletop marked the birth of the modern oil
industry. Large corporations such as Exxon, Gulf, and
Texaco trace their origins to Spindletop. The fuel they
40   produced profoundly influenced American industry
and transportation, as well as the world we inhabit
today.

boomtowns:

④ Reread Reread lines 24–42. Why was Spindletop important in the history of Texas and the world? Cite details from the text in your answer.

_____

_____

_____

5 Read As you read, collect and cite text evidence.

- Circle the topic of Taylor Castillo's email.
- Underline the fact that Taylor shares.

We welcome input from our readers. Please e-mail us your comments!

From: TCastillo@beaumont.net
To: webmaster@texashistoryonline.com
CC:

Subject: | Spindletop

Dear Texas History Online,

    Here's an interesting fact I learned. In just two years after the Spindletop **gusher,** there were more than 600 oil companies with 285 churning oil wells in the Beaumont area. Some of those oil companies are still around!

    Thanks for the article.

    Taylor Castillo

    Grade 4

    Beaumont Hill School

gusher:

6 Reread and Discuss Reread Taylor's email. How does her "interesting fact" support the idea that Spindletop was the birthplace of the modern oil industry? Cite evidence from the text in your discussion.

SHORT RESPONSE

Cite Text Evidence What qualities did Higgins and Lucas have that helped them succeed in the oil business?

_____

_____

_____

_____

_____

_____

Background People and animals—dogs, especially—have worked together for thousands of years, but in the last few decades service animals have taken on even more critical roles in helping people. Animals now work as assistants for people with a wide range of disabilities. As this article describes, they can also come to the rescue when people are in trouble.

Setting a Purpose Read the text to learn how dogs can use their special abilities to do things people can't do.

Knowing Noses
Search-and-Rescue Dogs

Informational Text by Ellen Gold

CLOSE READ
Notes

(1) Read As you read, collect and cite text evidence.
- Underline details that tell why dogs are good at searching and rescuing.
- Circle details that tell the kinds of jobs SAR dogs do.

Search-and-rescue dogs are trained to perform some very special jobs. They often assist in finding someone who is lost. Sometimes they help police officers solve crimes such as

5　**burglaries.** These hard-working dogs are also known as SAR dogs. SAR stands for "Search And Rescue."

burglaries:

Noses to the Rescue!

Dogs have a great sense of smell. They have about twenty-
five times more smell **receptors** than people have. This
10 makes them good at search-and-rescue work.
SAR dogs are trained to follow scents in the air, on the
ground, and even underwater!

Air-scent dogs are the most common type of SAR dog.
They can find a lost person by smelling the scent that
15 person has left behind. The dogs follow the scent as it gets
stronger. Then, they lead the rescuers to the lost person.

Qualities of a Good SAR Dog

SAR dog trainers look for certain qualities in dogs prior to
teaching them SAR skills. They look for dogs that like to
play and like to please their trainers. Dogs with these
20 qualities will respond to rewards when being trained. SAR
dogs should also be friendly, healthy, and smart. They
should not be afraid of strangers. Certain types of dogs have
a natural talent for search-and-rescue work. These are
usually bloodhounds, German shepherds, and golden
25 retrievers.

② **Reread** Reread lines 1–25. Summarize what makes a dog a good candidate
for SAR training and the kinds of jobs SAR dogs do.

_____

_____

_____

_____

SAR Training and Work

Training SAR dogs is a big job. It can take more than a year to get a dog ready for a search-and-rescue **mission**. Regrettably, some dogs that go through training don't have what it takes to be SAR dogs.

30   Those that do become SAR dogs deal with different types of jobs. Sometimes they search for a suspect who is part of a crime scheme. Often their searches help innocent people. They might search for someone lost in the wilderness or trapped in fallen buildings.

35   Whatever their mission might be, SAR dogs are a big help to their human teams.

mission:

The SAR Dog and the Lost Boy: A Happy Ending

In March of 2007, a twelve-year-old Boy Scout wandered away from his troop's campsite in North Carolina. He **misjudged** the seriousness of being alone in the wilderness

40 and soon found himself lost.

The boy survived for four days by drinking stream water and finding safe places to sleep. His father **speculated** that the boy was trying to live out his favorite story. It is about a boy who survives in the wilderness on his own.

45 Meanwhile, a search-and-rescue team with dogs was looking for the boy. One of the dogs, named Gandalf, picked up the boy's scent and found him. What a great favor Gandalf did for the boy and his family!

misjudged:

speculated:

---

④ Reread and Discuss Review the headings and the picture on the previous page. How do these text and graphic features help you understand what you're reading?

SHORT RESPONSE

Cite Text Evidence The text states that "SAR dogs are a big help to their human teams." Do you agree? Explain your answer, citing text evidence.

_____

_____

_____

_____

_____

Background "Zomo's Friends" is a folktale, a story that has been passed on through generations. The main character, Zomo, is a rabbit. He is a trickster, a character who tricks people to get what he wants. In this folktale, adages and proverbs—short sayings that tell a basic truth—help explain Zomo's problem and how he solves it.

Setting a Purpose Read the text to learn how a clever rabbit learns an important lesson about friendship.

Zomo's Friends

Folktale retold by Tamara Andrews
illustrated by Benjamin Bay

CLOSE READ
Notes

1 **Read** As you read, collect and cite text evidence.

- Circle the reason Zomo is not happy.
- Underline what the Sky God tells Zomo about why he doesn't have friends.
- Circle the Sky God's instructions for Zomo.

clever:

The best way to have a friend is to be one. Zomo the Rabbit didn't know that—he had to learn it for himself. Many animals lived in the jungle, and many were good friends to one another. Zomo thought he
5 was better than all the other animals, and he certainly thought he was more **clever.** He was the cleverest animal in the jungle. He was the cleverest animal in the land.

Zomo was quite proud of his cleverness. He often

10 boasted and bragged to the other animals, and he laughed
at his own many tricks. But as much as Zomo liked being
clever, he was not happy. The animals were tired of Zomo's
boasting and bragging. Not one of them wanted to be
Zomo's friend.

15   So Zomo the Rabbit went to talk to Sky God for advice.
He waited at the big rock in the jungle where he knew Sky
God often appeared.

"The animals don't trust you," Sky God told Zomo.
"They have all been **victims** of your tricks, and you have

20 lost their respect. If it's friendship you seek, you must earn
it. The only way to have friends is to be one yourself."

"What can I do to earn friendship?" Zomo asked Sky
God. "How can I earn the animals' trust?"

"Show them you can be trusted," said Sky God. "Bring

25 me the tail of the Zebra," ordered Sky God. Zebra lived in
the grasslands far away.

"Remember," warned Sky God, "cleverness is a gift, but
you must learn to use it wisely. Trickery can be used for
good, but trickery can also make others angry. You must

30 always do unto others as you would have others do unto
you."

victims:

---

② **Reread** Reread lines 1–31. What three adages or proverbs do you find? How do they relate to Zomo's problem?

_____

_____

_____

_____

_____

③ **Read** As you read, collect and cite text evidence.

- Underline text that describes what happens when Zomo begins to play his violin.
- Circle the text that tells what Zomo and Zebra do together.

Zomo was eager to start on his journey. He barely heard Sky God's words. Zomo hopped off to find Zebra in the grasslands to the west.

35 "Sun will guide me," Zomo said to himself. "He goes to sleep in the western ocean. If I keep my eye on Sun, I should have no trouble finding my way." Zomo followed Sun to the grasslands. Sun kept moving west. Zomo waved goodbye as Sun sank in the deep, blue water to

40 sleep soundly beneath the waves.

Zomo did not feel sleepy. He had far too much to do. The sky was black, and the grasslands before him appeared endless. "I'm sure that Zebra is hiding from me!" he thought. "I can't see through the darkness!

45 Zebra could be just around the corner, or he could be hiding far, far away."

At first, Zomo decided that he'd wait for morning and ask Sun to help him find Zebra. "Zebra can't hide from the light of Sun's day!" Zomo reasoned. Just then,

50 though, he remembered Sky God's words. "If I am going to gain Zebra's trust," thought Zomo, "I should not use tricks or **shortcuts.** I will have to search for Zebra all by myself."

Zomo walked through the grasslands and began to

55 play his violin. The music awakened Zebra, who listened and began to dance.

shortcuts:

As he played, Zomo watched Zebra move with grace amid the tall grass. "Why Zebra!" Zomo called out. "How lovely! How did you learn to dance?"

60 Zebra stopped dancing. Zomo stopped playing.

"I learned to dance from my father," said Zebra. "He was the greatest dancer in the jungle and the greatest dancer in all the land. When my father danced, the rain fell softly from the sky." Zebra **swayed** this way and that way, gliding

65 across the grasslands. He reached for Zomo's hand.

Together, they glided from left to right. Hand in hand, they danced until Sun appeared again. They smiled as a soft warm rain fell from the clouds and watered the land.

Zomo said goodbye to Zebra. He hopped back to find

70 Sky God.

"Did you bring me the tail of Zebra?" asked Sky God.

"Indeed I did," Zomo replied. "And what a beautiful tale it is!" Zomo shared the lovely tale of Zebra and the rain dance.

75 Sky God smiled. "I am glad to see that you are learning how to be clever without playing tricks. You have brought back a tale and made a friend in the grasslands. That is good, but just a start."

Zomo barely heard these words as he thought happily

80 about his dance with Zebra in the soft rain.

swayed:

---

4 Reread Reread lines 54–75. What details make the Sky God think that Zomo has made a friend?

_____

_____

_____

_____

5 Read As you read, collect and cite text evidence.

- Underline what Sky God asks Zomo to bring next.
- Circle the details that tell how Crocodile responds to Zomo.

"Remember, Zomo," said Sky God, "you are clever, and cleverness is a gift. It is said, A little rain each day will fill the rivers to overflowing. If it's further friendship you seek, you must do more to earn it. Bring
85 me the tears of the Crocodile." Sky God waved goodbye to the rabbit and disappeared into the clouds.

Zomo waved back, and once again he began a long hop. He followed a winding path through the jungle and arrived at a great swamp. In the middle of the water lay
90 Crocodile, fast asleep.

"Hey, Croc!" shouted Zomo. "It's morning! Don't you think it's time to wake up?" Crocodile opened his eyes angrily. The last thing he wanted to see was Zomo. He took one look and snapped his eyes shut.

95 "I have a story to tell you," said Zomo. "It's really a beautiful tale." He started talking, but Croc kept his eyes shut. Zomo shared the tale of Zebra and the rain dance. He told about how Zebra's dancing made the rain fall from the clouds. Finally, Croc began to listen, wide
100 awake!

6 Reread and Discuss Reread lines 91–100. Discuss how Croc's mood changes and why it does. Cite details from the text in your discussion.

7 Read As you read, collect and cite text evidence.

- Underline the details that tell how Zomo collects Croc's tears.
- Circle Sky God's next task for Zomo.

"Aha! I have your **attention,**" said Zomo. "Now I can show you the dance." Zomo began to dance, but not like he danced with Zebra. He did not glide—he hopped. He did not sway—he fell. He fell into the water near Crocodile. His
105 hat landed upside down.

Crocodile laughed and laughed. Zomo began laughing, too. Crocodile laughed so hard he cried big crocodile tears. The tears dripped from his eyes and fell into Zomo's hat.

Zomo felt very clever indeed. He waved goodbye to
110 Crocodile and walked the long way back to Sky God. Once again, Sky God was **impressed.**

"So now you have a friend in the grasslands," said Sky God. "You have Crocodile's friendship, too. You made them smile and laugh, but these animals are not happy. They
115 won't be happy at all until someone brings back the Moon."

Zomo had forgotten about the Moon. The Moon had been stolen years ago, and the night sky had grown very dark. "I brought back the tale of Zebra," thought Zomo. "I brought back Crocodile's tears, too. I can bring back the
120 Moon—I know it. I am the cleverest animal in the jungle. I am the cleverest animal in all the land."

attention:

impressed:

ditch:

Zomo set out once again, this time to look for the Moon. He walked deep into the jungle and searched for the deepest **ditch.** Before long, he found it. He peered

125 inside, and just as he suspected, he saw a faint white ball glowing beneath the dirt.

Zomo wasted no time. He was sure he had found the Moon. He tipped over his hat, which was quite heavy with Croc's tears, and emptied it into the ditch. As the

130 water in the ditch got higher and higher, the Moon floated to the surface. Zomo lifted it from the water and tossed it up in the sky.

8 Reread Reread lines 127–132. Explain how Zomo is able to put the Moon back in the sky. Use the picture and cite details from the story in your answer.

_____

_____

_____

_____

_____

9 Read As you read, collect and cite text evidence.

- Underline the things the animals shout when they look up at the sky.
- Circle the lesson Zomo learns.

The animals came out from their hidden homes in the jungle. One by one, they looked up at the sky. Suddenly, the

135 animals began shouting! "Hooray for Zomo!" shouted Casey the Camel. "Friend to us all," said Glinda the Goat.

Zomo felt more clever than ever. He felt better than ever, too. It was great to be clever, but it was even better to have friends. It seemed all of the animals were now Zomo's

140 friends. He remembered an old saying that was kind of clever: *You can never have enough friends.*

10 Reread and Discuss Reread lines 133–140. Discuss why the animals are ready to be friends with Zomo.

SHORT RESPONSE

Cite Text Evidence Find the adage at the end of the story. How does it apply to Zomo and everything that has happened to him in the story? Cite text evidence in your response.

_____

_____

_____

_____

_____

_____

Background What is one way to learn about the environment and about healthy eating? By planting a garden, of course! In this text, you will read about how one program is teaching kids to get their hands dirty—and to cook some tasty food, too.

Setting a Purpose Read the text to learn how one school helps students learn through growing a garden.

The Edible Schoolyard

Informational Text by Ned L. Legol

CLOSE READ
Notes

① Read As you read, collect and cite text evidence.

- Circle text that describes what students have to do as part of the program.
- Underline text that describes what students learn.
- Circle the name of the person who started the program.

founded:

The Edible Schoolyard program is part garden, part kitchen, and part classroom. It is all about the joy of learning. The large garden is right behind Martin Luther King, Jr. Middle School in
5   Berkeley, California. Chef Alice Waters **founded** The Edible Schoolyard. She likes to dedicate a lot of her time to it.

86

Inside the Edible Schoolyard

Every year, the school's sixth-grade students plant, tend, and harvest the crops from the garden. They learn about the
10 effects that changing climate and weather have on the plants. During a drought, for example, they must water the garden more often. This keeps everything alive and healthy.

The students grow many types of fruits, vegetables, and herbs. Brilliant colors surround the kids as they work in the
15 garden that stretches toward the horizon.

Time to Get Cooking

The students also learn how to cook healthy meals with the food they grow. The school houses many different students and cultures. So, the meals vary from Indian curries to Mediterranean grape leaves. Some of the kids learn to
20 overcome their fear of unknown foods.

If there are conflicts in the kitchen or the garden, students must work to solve them. The program fits with Martin Luther King, Jr.'s vision of **inclusion,** equality, and peaceful growth without violence.

inclusion:

2 **Reread** Reread lines 8–24. Summarize what the Edible Schoolyard teaches students.

_____

_____

_____

_____

_____

3 Read As you read, collect and cite text evidence.

- Circle the amount of vegetables and fruits a person should eat every day.
- Underline details that explain why the Edible Schoolyard has gotten good publicity.
- Circle the name of another organization that teaches kids about healthy eating.

Healthy Eating

According to the U.S. government, people should eat the following kinds and amounts of food each day.

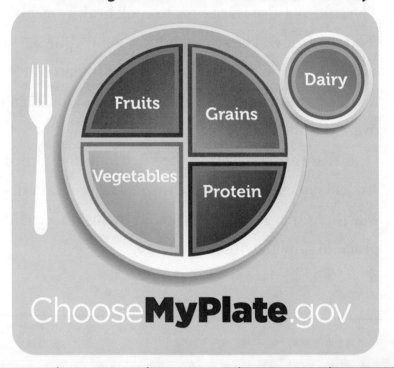

ChooseMyPlate.gov

Grains	Vegetables	Fruits	Dairy	Protein
6 oz	2.5 cups	2 cups	3 cups	5.5 oz

Measurement: oz = ounces

Source: United States Department of Agriculture

Tastes Great and Is Healthy Too

25 The Edible Schoolyard program has received good publicity for teaching students about healthy food. Everything grown in the garden is **organic.** All meals the kids prepare are good for them.

Many other groups, such as The American Dietetic
30 Association, also teach kids and adults about eating healthy. Because it is so important, a healthy school lunch is something that is often talked about in every state capitol.

organic:

(4) Reread and Discuss Reread lines 25–32. What can you infer about the kinds of food that are healthy? Cite evidence from the text in your discussion.

SHORT RESPONSE

Cite Text Evidence How does the pie chart support ideas in the text? Cite details from the text in your response.

_____

_____

_____

_____

_____

Background Have relatives ever told you stories about your family and its history? Some Native American stories have been passed down through generations in the form of poems. They help Native American groups teach their children about their culture, their history, and the things they most value.

Setting a Purpose Read the text and the poems to learn how poetry reflects Native American ideas about nature.

Native American Nature Poetry

Poetry

© Houghton Mifflin Harcourt Publishing Company • Image Credits: ©Buddy Mays/Corbis

CLOSE READ
Notes

① Read As you read, collect and cite text evidence.

- Underline two themes in Native American poetry.
- Circle text that describes how Native American poems and stories were passed down.
- Underline text that describes how some poems and stories were preserved in the late 1800s.

Nature and a person's relationship to nature are two important themes in Native American poetry. A poem might include details that describe a common place, such as a forest with
5   wind rustling through the trees. It might personify an object, giving human characteristics to it. Then again, a poem might tell what is important in life.

Preserving Oral Traditions

For centuries Native Americans passed their poems, songs,
10 and stories **orally** from one generation to the next. People
who did not speak Native American languages needed an
interpreter to help them understand and write down these
stories.

By the late 1800s, people could use cylinder recorders
15 to record and play sounds. Compared to today's small
electronic recorders, cylinder recorders were clumsy to use.
Yet they **preserved** sounds exactly. In 1890 this recorder
became important to scientist Jesse Fewkes, who was asked
to accompany a corps of researchers to the southwestern
20 United States. The cylinder recorder was among Fewkes's
supplies. He used it to record and preserve Native American
oral stories.

orally:

preserved:

2 Reread Reread lines 9–22. Summarize the different ways that Native
American poems and stories have been preserved.

_____

_____

_____

_____

_____

③ Read As you read, collect and cite text evidence.

- Circle what the speaker in the Nootka poem and the moon in the Teton Sioux poem each tell readers to do.
- Underline words and phrases that describe the wind.

Untitled
Nootka

behold:

You, whose day it is,
Make it beautiful.
Get out your rainbow colors,
So it will be beautiful.

Untitled
Teton Sioux

Here am I
Behold me
It said as it rose,
I am the moon
5 Behold me.

The Wind
Crow

At night,
The wind keeps us awake,
Rustling through the trees.
We don't know how we'll get to sleep,
5 Until we do—
Dropping off as suddenly
As the wind dying down.

④ Reread Reread the three poems. What can you infer about what these Native American groups value? Cite details from the text in your answer.

_____

_____

_____

_____

- Circle text that describes the speaker's small adventures.
- Underline what the speaker says is the most important thing.

I Think Over Again
My Small Adventures

Anonymous
(North American Indian;
nineteenth century)

I think over again my small adventures,

My fears,

Those small ones that seemed so big,

For all the **vital** things

5   I had to get and to reach;

And yet there is only one great thing,

The only thing,

To live to see the great day that dawns

And the light that fills the world.

vital:

6 **Reread and Discuss** Reread the poem. Discuss what the speaker means by "the vital things / I had to get and to reach." How does it contrast with what the speaker calls the "one great thing"? Cite evidence from the text in your discussion.

SHORT RESPONSE

Cite Text Evidence In what way is this poem also about nature? Cite text evidence in your response.

_____

_____

_____

_____

UNIT 5
Change It Up

Background The average young person sees about 40,000 television ads each year, and lots more in magazines and online. Some people worry that these ads encourage kids to buy stuff they don't need and even stuff that's bad for them, like junk food. Being a critical viewer of ads can help you avoid being influenced in ways you don't want.

Setting a Purpose Read the text and analyze the posters to learn about the persuasive techniques advertisers use.

Make the Switch

Advertisements

CLOSE READ
Notes

① **Read** As you read, collect and cite text evidence.

- Underline the main purpose or goal of all ads.
- Circle two ways in which ads can present ideas to viewers.

How many ads do you see on an average day? Chances are you see hundreds of them. They may be on billboards, T-shirts, and buses, in stores and magazines, and, of course, on television.

5   Ads may be selling a product, a service, or an idea, but they all have one thing in common. Their goal is to influence you. Ads use a combination of **techniques** to do this. Often they introduce ideas not just with words but with pictures and colors.

10   Be aware of the persuasive techniques used in ads. Sometimes ads try to convince you to do things you were not aware of or even things that you didn't want to do at all! On the following pages are two posters

15   for you to study. How do they try to influence your thoughts and behavior?

techniques:

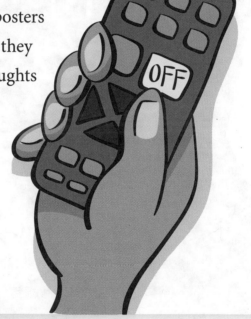

② **Reread** Reread lines 1–13. Why is it important to analyze the ads you see? What are some things to look out for? Cite evidence from the text in your answer.

_____

_____

_____

_____

_____

③ **Read** As you read, collect and cite text evidence.

- Underline text that describes the colors in each poster.
- Circle words that help persuade viewers to agree with each poster's message.

nocturnal:

The goal of this poster is to make you appreciate the joys of activity.

The colors in this poster are very bright. The colors can help turn ordinary activities into great feats of adventure.

The drawings show movement and look lively. They show that the effort of finding something else to do will be **rewarding.**

rewarding:

④ Reread and Discuss How do the people shown in the two posters feel? How do you know? Cite details from the posters in your discussion.

SHORT RESPONSE

Cite Text Evidence What message are both posters trying to communicate? What techniques does each poster use to get this message across? Cite details from the posters in your response.

_____

_____

_____

_____

Background The Constitution was written after the colonies gained independence from Britain. It was finally ratified, or approved, in 1790. The Constitution can be changed, although a change or amendment is difficult to make. It has been done only 27 times since the Constitution became the law of the land.

Setting a Purpose Read the text to learn how the Constitution establishes the government and protects people's rights.

The Role of the Constitution

Informational Text by Carl DeSoto

CLOSE READ
Notes

① **Read** As you read, collect and cite text evidence.
- Underline text that describes what the U.S. Constitution does.
- Circle text that describes what a state constitution does.

The Constitution

A constitution is a plan of government. A government is a system of leaders and laws by which a community, state, or nation is governed. The United States Constitution sets up the
5 national government. It says that all citizens should be treated fairly by government. It says that their freedom should be protected.

Each state has a state constitution that sets up the government for that state. A state constitution must obey
10 the United States Constitution. It cannot take away rights **granted** by the United States Constitution.

granted:

The Constitution sets up the United States government as a democracy, which means that the people elect leaders to govern them. The government gets its power from the
15 people, so it is a **republic.** Citizens elect leaders to represent them in government.

republic:

The Three Branches

The United States Constitution organizes the national government into three branches, or parts. These three branches are the legislative branch, the executive branch,
20 and the judicial branch. Likewise, each state has a government divided into these three branches. The Constitution tells what each branch of the government can and cannot do.

2 Reread Reread lines 4–23. Summarize the difference between the role of the U.S. Constitution and that of state constitutions.

_____

_____

_____

_____

③ **Read** As you read, collect and cite text evidence.

- Circle the office or governing body in each branch of the federal government.
- Underline the office or governing body in each state.
- Underline rights and freedoms in the Bill of Rights.

Branches of the Federal Government		
Legislative Branch	**Executive Branch**	**Judicial Branch**
• Makes national laws • Made up of Senate and House of Representatives	• Enforces national laws • Led by President of the United States	• Makes sure laws agree with the Constitution • Made up of Supreme Court and other courts

The Legislative Branch

The legislative branch of government makes laws that
25 the entire nation must follow. Congress is the main body
of the legislative branch. Congress is made up of two
parts: the Senate and the House of Representatives. The
Senate has two senators elected from each state—one
hundred in all. The number of representatives elected
30 from each state depends on the state's population. The
more **residents** a state has, the more representatives it is
allowed to elect to the House of Representatives. All
states, except Nebraska, also have a legislative branch
made up of a state senate and a house of representatives.
35 Nebraska has just one house.

The Executive Branch

The executive branch carries out the laws made by
Congress. The President of the United States is the leader
of the executive branch. When the President takes office,
he or she promises to preserve, protect, and defend the
40 Constitution of the United States. At the state level, the
leader of the executive branch is the governor.

residents:

The Judicial Branch

The judicial branch is made up of the Supreme Court as well as other courts. The Supreme Court is the nation's highest court. It is made up of nine judges, called justices.

45 The justices are chosen by the President and approved by Congress. The justices make sure laws agree with the Constitution and are carried out fairly. Similarly, each state has a judicial branch made up of a state supreme court and various other courts.

Rights and Freedoms

50 The United States Constitution provides rights and freedoms for American citizens. The Bill of Rights is a part of the Constitution. It lists the many rights and freedoms of American citizens. These freedoms include freedom of the **press,** freedom of speech, and freedom of religion. It also

55 protects Americans accused of crimes by giving them the right to a trial by **jury.**

CLOSE READ
Notes

press:

jury:

4 **Reread** Reread lines 24–49. Summarize the role of each branch of the U.S. government.

_____

_____

_____

_____

_____

(5) **Read** As you read, collect and cite text evidence.

• Circle the duties of U.S. citizens.

• Underline services provided by the government.

One important right is the right to choose leaders and make decisions by majority rule. Under the Constitution, each citizen who is at least 18 years old gets
60 one vote in an election. The winner is the person or idea that gets the most votes.

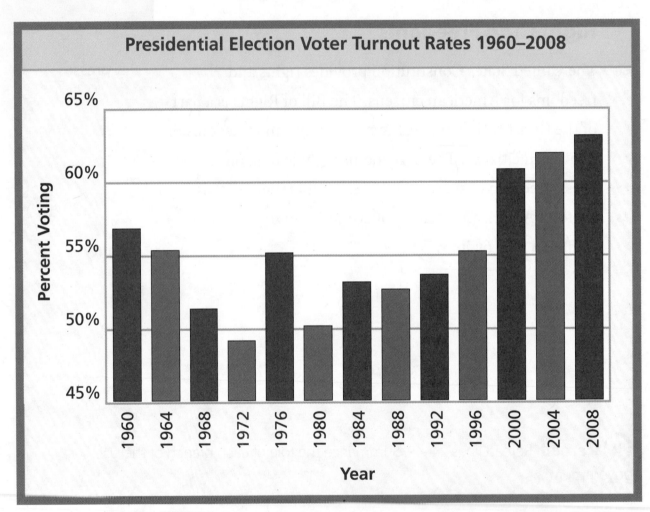

Presidential Election Voter Turnout Rates 1960–2008

The graph shows the percentage of people eligible to vote who actually voted in presidential elections from 1960 to 2008. In most years, more than half of eligible voters did their duty by voting to elect the President. In recent years, more than 60% of eligible voters cast ballots, or voted.

Duties of Citizens

Americans' rights are balanced by duties. For example, the right to choose leaders is balanced by the duty to vote. The right to a jury trial is balanced by the duty to serve on a

65   jury.

    The government provides services for American citizens. It **maintains** the military to protect the country in times of war. It helps people rebuild their communities after natural disasters. In return, citizens have the duty to pay taxes. The

70   money from taxes pays for the costs of running the government. The Constitution gives the government the right to collect taxes.

maintains:

---

6 **Reread and Discuss** Reread lines 62–72. What might happen if either the government or the citizens did not fulfill their duties? Cite evidence from the text in your discussion.

SHORT RESPONSE

Cite Text Evidence How does the graph on page 104 support the idea that the majority of people take at least one of their duties as citizens seriously? Cite details from the text in your response.

_____

_____

_____

_____

Background Imagine a tree as tall as a 30-story skyscraper. That's how tall some coast redwoods are. These giants grow this tall only on California's northern coast, where they thrive in the cool, rainy climate. How long does a tree take to reach such a height? Hundreds, even thousands of years!

Setting a Purpose Read the text to understand how one towering tree grew and changed.

Towering Trees

Poetry

CLOSE READ
Notes

① Read As you read, collect and cite text evidence.

- Circle references to time.
- Underline examples of personification, in which human qualities are given to the tree.

majesty:

The poem "First Recorded 6,000-Year-Old Tree in America" describes the **majesty** of towering trees. Specifically, it is about the Eon Tree, a coast redwood located in Humboldt County,

5   California. This amazing tree was 250 feet tall and was estimated to be 6,200 years old.

First Recorded 6,000-Year-Old Tree in America

by J. Patrick Lewis

When Mother Nature held her ground,

When almost no one was around,

A redwood **bud** began to grow

And watch the seasons come and go.

bud:

5 For sixty centuries or more,

It stood upon the forest floor

And waved its arms about the sky

And sang a woodland lullaby.

December 1977;

10 The Eon Tree, so tall to heaven,

Bowed gracefully and **bid** farewell

bid:

To all its fellow trees,

and fell.

---

(2) Reread and Discuss Reread the poem. How do you think the speaker feels about what happened to the tree in December 1977? Cite text evidence.

SHORT RESPONSE

Cite Text Evidence   How does the poet's use of personification help you picture the tree? Cite evidence from the text in your response.

_____

_____

_____

_____

_____

_____

Background National Marine Sanctuaries were first created in 1972 to protect unique areas in the sea and in the Great Lakes. But these protected areas are open to everyone. They provide important places for scientists to do research. They are also popular places for people to visit.

Setting a Purpose Read the text to learn how plants and animals in a sea sanctuary depend on each other.

Sea Sanctuary

Informational Text by Rob Hale

CLOSE READ
Notes

1 **Read** As you read, collect and cite text evidence.

- Underline text that describes how all the parts of an ecosystem work together.
- Circle text that describes why so many species are found in Monterey Bay.

sanctuary:

We often think of a wildlife **sanctuary** as a jewel of land that has been set aside to keep safe. But there are ocean sanctuaries, too. The United States government has preserved thirteen

5   important areas as marine, or sea, sanctuaries. The largest of them is California's Monterey Bay National Marine Sanctuary.

This sanctuary is an ecosystem. It is an environment whose nonliving parts, such as water and earth, work with its living parts. Each part is like a **companion** to another part. "Upwelling" is one example of this. Wind causes cold water to rise to the surface of the ocean. This cold water causes new plants to grow. Then, animals come to eat these plants. This food source is the chief reason why so many species are drawn to Monterey Bay. No enclosure, or closed space, keeps them there. The food does!

companion:

A sea otter finds plenty of shellfish to eat in Monterey Bay. These animals suffered a drop in numbers because of being hunted for their fur in the early 1900s. Now, they are slowly starting to return to the area.

②Reread Reread lines 8–16. Summarize the way in which the living and nonliving parts of Monterey Bay work together.

_____

_____

_____

_____

3 **Read** As you read, collect and cite text evidence.

- Underline text that describes what a food chain is.
- Circle the kinds of animals that might be found in Flower Garden Banks.

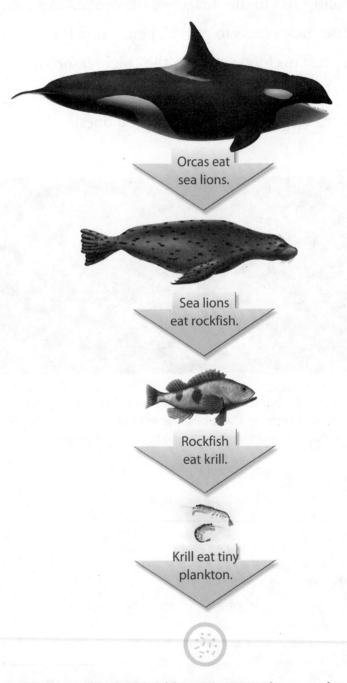

Orcas eat sea lions.

Sea lions eat rockfish.

Rockfish eat krill.

Krill eat tiny plankton.

Predators and Prey A healthy environment keeps each member of the food chain well fed. Orcas eat sea lions, sea lions eat rockfish, and so on down to tiny plankton.

Seafood Chain

Each plant and animal in a sanctary is part of a food chain.
A necessary bond connects each hunter to its prey. The
need for food is why a hungry orca might charge at a sea

20 lion. It is the same reason a sea lion might leave a rockfish
exhausted after a chase. One animal depends on another for
life.

Flower Garden Banks

Coral reefs and ocean waters are inseparable. Coral reefs
can be found 110 miles off the Texas and Louisiana coasts.

25 They are protected by the Flower Garden Banks, a 36,000-
acre marine sanctuary.

    The coral reefs lie on top of two salt domes, old
underwater mountains. Today Flower Garden Banks
Sanctuary is home to twenty-three types of coral. Anyone

30 with affection for marine creatures will find many animals
there. One might see turtles, manta rays, or the odd
intruder, such as the huge whale shark.

coral reefs:

④ Reread and Discuss Reread lines 17–22. How does the diagram on
page 110 support the ideas in this text? Cite specific details in your discussion.

SHORT RESPONSE

Cite Text Evidence   Why might Flower Garden Banks have become a marine
sanctuary? Cite evidence from the text in your response.

_____

_____

_____

_____

Background We live in a time of great invention. Just fifty years ago, home computers were far in the future, and portable phones didn't seem possible. Cars have been around for more than a hundred years, but we can still only dream about owning cars that fly.

Setting a Purpose Read the text to learn about flying cars, from the earliest models to today's designs.

The Flying Car

Informational Text by Vanessa Walker

CLOSE READ
Notes

(1) **Read** As you read, collect and cite text evidence.

- Underline the goals of flying car inventors.
- Circle the problem with each early model.

afford:

If you think that flying cars are science fiction, think again. For decades, inventors have been building cars that can also fly. Their goal is to make a flying car that many people can **afford,**
5   one that is not too difficult to fly and is also safe. But the history of flying cars proves that this goal is also quite a challenge.

The Earliest Flying Cars

The first flying cars never quite made it off the ground. In 1841, steam engines powered trains and ships. One inventor

10 thought that steam engines could also be used to power a flying car. The car's wings were 150 feet long—about half as long as a football field. The car, with its **bulky** engine and huge wings, never flew.

bulky:

After the steam engine,

15 serious attempts at building a flying car slowed down for a few years. Then, in 1917, Glenn Curtiss introduced a flying car that seated three

20 people. Curtiss could not actually get his car in the air for very long. Instead, the car

HENSON'S AERIAL STEAM CARRIAGE.

made short hops, staying in flight only briefly. He made plans to improve the car and **eventually** sell it to the public,

eventually:

25 but World War I put those plans on hold. Curtiss's flying car never reached the skies.

Even Henry Ford, who had great success manufacturing the first automobiles, tried to build a flying car. In 1926, Ford rolled out his **version** of a car that could fly. But Ford,

version:

30 too, gave up when the flying car he was testing crashed.

② **Reread** Reread lines 8–30. What was the problem with the earliest flying cars? Cite text details in your answer.

_____

_____

_____

③ **Read** As you read, collect and cite text evidence.

- Circle the year of each flying car in "Taking to the Skies."
- Underline details of each machine's design.
- Circle the two main designs for current models.

Taking to the Skies

Finally, in 1937, a flying car actually took off and flew some distance. The Aerobile had car parts, including a car engine. It also had removable wings so that the car could be driven on the road. When it was time for
35   takeoff, the pilot simply had to reattach the wings. Five of these cars were built. You can still see one of them today at the National Museum of Air and Space in Washington, D.C. However, you won't see the Aerobile on the road. Like the flying cars that came before it, the
40   Aerobile was never sold to the public.

featured:

Perhaps one of the strangest-looking flying cars rolled down the runway in 1947. This flying car **featured** a tail section of an airplane and 36-foot wings attached to the body of a car. The machine made two successful
45   flights, staying in the air above San Diego for more than an hour. But on the third flight, it crashed. So did its inventor's hopes for a flying car that he could sell to consumers.

Since 1947, there have been many other attempts at
50   building safe, affordable flying cars. Even the U.S. military attempted to build one. In 1958, the army built a flying jeep to move weapons over and around mountains. The jeep had rotors like a helicopter, so the machine could go between buildings and under trees,

hovering:

55   **hovering** just feet off the ground. It could also fly several

thousand feet high. When it landed, it came down on a
tricycle tire that acted as landing gear. The Airgeep made its
first successful flight in 1962. However, the army decided
against building more of them. Instead, they turned to
60   helicopters to **transport** weapons and soldiers.

transport:

The Flying Car of Tomorrow

Inventors have not given up on building a flying car that is
safe and easy to use. And companies have not given up on
the idea of building a flying car that they can sell to the
public. In fact, several companies in the United States and
65   Europe are developing cars that they plan to put on the
market in the next few years.

There are two main designs for the flying cars that are
now being built. Some are designed like a plane so that they
can take off on a runway. These cars have wings that can be
70   folded with the push of a button. They can fly hundreds of
miles and are powered with the same fuel used for a regular
car. The idea is that you would drive your car to the airport,
unfold your wings, and take off.

Other flying cars have been designed for vertical liftoff.
75   This means that instead of rolling down a runway, the car
simply rises into the air like a helicopter. Though it sounds
like a great way to get out of traffic, these cars could not
take off on a road. They would need to be driven to an
airport because they create too much wind during liftoff.
80   Inventors hope to build a flying car soon that could take off
and land anywhere—on a city street or in a big field.

④ Reread and Discuss Reread lines 31–60. Discuss the different designs
and any reasons they might not work well in the real world. Cite evidence from the
text in your discussion.

⑤ Read As you read, collect and cite text evidence.

- Circle the three key problems still to be solved before flying cars will be sold to consumers.
- Underline questions that need to be answered before people can fly cars.

manufacture:

The Problem with Flying Cars

If there have been so many flying cars, why aren't we seeing them in the skies? One answer is cost. For a company to **manufacture** a flying car, it must have

85   many customers waiting to buy one. The cost of a flying car is expected to be more than $200,000—much more than the cost of the average earthbound car. It's also much more than most people can afford. Companies that are making flying cars are trying to bring the cost

90   down, hoping to attract more customers when they do finally begin selling their cars.

Pollution is another problem with flying cars. The cars that have been built use a lot of fuel. This is expensive and creates air pollution. The engines also

95   create noise pollution, both when they take off and when they buzz overhead. Imagine a sky full of flying cars, engines roaring, and you might not be so excited to see them take off.

© Houghton Mifflin Harcourt Publishing Company • Image Credits: ©ZUMA Press, Inc./Alamy

The biggest problem, however, is safety. People have been

100 able to build flying cars. They have even been able to keep them in the air. But the government must first decide if the cars are safe, not just for the pilot but also for people on the ground. With regular cars, you can pull over to the side of the road if something goes wrong. Pulling over is not so

105 easy if the engine in your flying car breaks down.

The companies that make flying cars are working on these problems. They hope to roll out a safe flying car, one that is quieter and doesn't use too much fuel, within the next few years. And they already have a few customers

110 lining up to buy them. Of course, if flying cars really do take off, there are other **concerns.** For example, will they be allowed to fly anywhere? Or will there be special "skyways," routes that flying cars must stay on? Will you need a special **license** to pilot a flying car? Will the cars have to fly at a

115 certain altitude, or distance above the ground? We may have answers to these questions very soon.

concerns:

license:

6 Reread and Discuss Reread lines 82–116. What solutions can you come up with for the problems listed? Support your ideas with logical reasons and facts.

SHORT RESPONSE

Cite Text Evidence   What is one problem current inventors face that the earliest inventors didn't have to think about? What is one problem that still exists? Cite text evidence in your response.

_____

_____

_____

_____

UNIT 6
Paths to Discovery

Background Did you know there are 37,000 different species of spiders in the world? One thousand of those are found in North America. Spiders, like scorpions, are arachnids. They have eight legs and their body is divided into two segments. Though some spiders are poisonous, most are helpful because they eat insect pests.

Setting a Purpose Read the text to discover how one boy changes his mind about spiders.

The Girl Who Loved Spiders

Realistic Fiction by Karen Halvorsen Schreck

CLOSE READ
Notes

1 Read As you read, collect and cite text evidence.

- Circle text that explains why Luis is afraid of spiders.
- Underline text that describes what Luis does that shows he is afraid of spiders.

I hate spiders. That's the first thing you should know about me.

My mom and I just moved from New York to Florida. That's the second thing you should know
5   about me. We moved because my mom got a new teaching job at a university here.

Before we moved, my best friend, Billy, told me all kinds of creepy stories about spiders that live in Florida.

"My brother knows a guy from there who got bitten by a brown **recluse** spider," Billy said. "This guy was *smart* about spiders, too. He shook out his shoes. He watched his step. His bite healed, but it was the *worst*."

Mom has told me it takes three weeks to make a habit.

15   It's only been a week since we moved, but I've already made one.

First thing every morning, I shake out my sneakers. Second thing, I put on my sneakers, though I'm still wearing pajamas. Third thing, I always watch my step.

20   Hey! Not one, but three new habits.

I blame them all on Billy.

I find Mom in the kitchen, drinking a glass of orange juice.

"You're awake, Luis? It's the crack of dawn!"

25   "Too hot."

Mom laughs. "It's summer. Aren't those winter pajamas?"

I don't tell her that flannel is better protection from spiders.

CLOSE READ
Notes

recluse:

(2) **Reread** Reread lines 14–29. Summarize what Luis does to avoid being bitten by a spider.

_____

_____

_____

_____

3 Read As you read, collect and cite text evidence.

- Circle what Luis sees as he jumps on the trampoline.
- Underline details that describe what the girl is doing in her backyard.
- Circle details that explain what happens when Luis surprises the girl.

30 Over breakfast, Mom discusses her plan for the day. It's the same as yesterday's: unpack and settle in.

"Oh!" Mom sits up straight in her chair. "I found a dead scorpion yesterday. It was in perfect shape—not a leg missing. Fascinating, really. I saved it in case you

35 wanted to see."

I gulp. "No thanks."

Great. **Venomous** spiders *and* scorpions.

venomous:

Mom shrugs. "Okay. So what are you up to?"

"TV?"

40 Mom frowns.

"There's always the trampoline," I mutter.

Mom bought the trampoline the day after we arrived. It's as big and bouncy as can be—something I always wanted that Billy had. I just wish Billy were here now to

45 teach me how to do a flip.

Not even 8:30 in the morning, and I'm on the trampoline again. Every jump takes me higher and higher.

In mid-air, I see her —two yards over—a girl about

50 my age. I keep jumping. The girl kneels before a bush, in tall grass where all kinds of biting and stinging things might be. She stays very still.

Next jump, I see something in her hands . . . a pink ball? Jump higher!

55　The girl claps the ball. Poof! A white cloud explodes from between her fingers.

I collapse onto the trampoline and scramble down. This I have to see. As I enter her yard, where the grass is taller, I freeze.

60　The ball in the girl's hands is a rolled-up sock. A camera dangles from a strap around her neck. She carefully settles the sock on the grass. Then she raises the camera and **peers** through it. I look where she's looking, at a delicate shape against the bush's leaves, like lace against green velvet.

peers:

65　The shape is a gigantic spider web, whitened by whatever the girl clapped from the sock.

"Yikes!" I yell at the sight of the web.

The girl cries out, surprised, and falls into the web. She springs up, web clinging to her.

70　"What's the big idea?" she shouts.

"Um . . . I was warning you! Guess you don't know about brown recluse spiders?"

"Of course I do. I've been trying to find one. They're shy, like most arachnids. I've found rarer breeds, even the
75　**burrowing** wolf spider. Still haven't tracked down a brown recluse." She points at the bush. "That was a common orb weaver. I've been watching her for days, until she got her web just right." The girl glares. "It sure was pretty—until you came along. Who are you, anyway?"

80　"Luis. I just moved here."

Not all spiders make their homes in webs. Some dig burrows.

burrowing:

④ Reread and Discuss Reread lines 55–80. Discuss how Luis and the girl differ on their feelings about spiders. Cite details from the text to support your ideas.

⑤ **Read** As you read, collect and cite text evidence.

- Underline text that explains Ashanti's goal.
- Circle why Luis and his mom go to Ashanti's house.
- Underline details that show Ashanti's interest in spiders.

safari:

"My name is Ashanti. Welcome to the neighborhood." She still sounds mad.

I cross my arms over my chest. "So you're on a spider **safari.** Why?"

85 "This summer my goal is to photograph one hundred spiders. I've always loved folktales about Anansi, a true spider-man. Spiders are cool."

I don't think before I say, "No, they aren't. Spiders are disgusting."

90 At that, Ashanti stalks away.

That afternoon Mom drives me to a park. "Never mind the heat," she says. "There'll be boys your age."

There's a decent playground, but a sign reads: BEWARE OF SNAKES! Where there are snakes,

95 there must be spiders. Ashanti would be in heaven. As for me . . .

wilts:

There are no boys my age. Two little girls sweat it out on the slide. Mom **wilts** on a bench. We drive home.

As we turn onto our street, we see Ashanti crouching

100 by a flower pot in her front yard. A woman kneels beside her.

alumni:

To my horror, Mom stops the car and gets out. Mom and Mrs. Smith, Ashanti's mom, hit it off. Mrs. Smith teaches at the university, too. Mr. Smith works for the

105 **alumni** office. Ashanti and I might be in the same fifth-grade class!

"Ashanti just found her first colorful crab spider," Mrs. Smith says. "It's the fiftieth spider she's photographed for her collection."

110 Mom and Mrs. Smith keep talking. Ashanti photographs her spider. I trace circles in the dirt. Then Mrs. Smith asks Mom and me over for dinner. Mom agrees.

Yippee.

115 Ashanti rolls her eyes. She's not exactly thrilled, either.

At six o'clock we're standing on the Smiths' front porch. Ashanti opens the door, and soon we sit down to dinner. The Smiths and Mom talk and laugh; Ashanti and I dig into
120 our lasagna. Soon my plate is empty; so is Ashanti's.

She gives me a **cautious** look. "Want to see Anansi?" she asks quietly, so as not to interrupt the grownups.

I shrug. "I guess."

Ashanti smiles a little. "Come on."

125 We go into the family room. African **artifacts** cover three of the walls: masks, instruments, weavings, and paintings. A large bulletin board hangs on the fourth wall. About fifty photographs of spiders are mounted there. I take a deep breath and go over to the board.

Many crab spiders use camouflage to catch prey.

cautious:

artifacts:

6 Reread Reread lines 107–129. How is Ashanti teaching Luis about spiders? Cite evidence from the text in your answer.

7 Read As you read, collect and cite text evidence.

- Underline details that show how Luis feels about spiders now.
- Circle text that shows that Luis's feelings about Ashanti have changed.

flexing:

130   I've got to admit, some of the spiders look pretty cool.

Ashanti points at a painting and says, "That's Anansi." I move closer to see a powerful-looking spider, standing upright, **flexing** six of its eight legs. The spider has a man's face . . . and eight eyes.

135   "Some legends say that Anansi created the sun, stars, and moon. Nice guy, huh?" Ashanti smiles. "He also could be tricky and greedy. In one story, he tries to keep all wisdom for himself."

Suddenly, Mrs. Smith calls from the kitchen,

140   "Ashanti! Quick! You've got to see this!"

Ashanti turns and runs from the room with me at her heels.

Mr. and Mrs. Smith are peering at a baseboard. Ashanti presses close.

145   "Brown recluse!" Mrs. Smith whispers.

Ashanti gasps in excitement. She grabs her camera and adjusts the settings. Mom holds me back, although Mrs. Smith reassures her that the spider won't hurt you if you don't hurt the spider. Just don't brush up against it.

150   "Ashanti knows what to do, Mom," I say.

© Houghton Mifflin Harcourt Publishing Company

Ashanti **glances** at me, surprised, and smiles. Then she adjusts the zoom on her camera and snaps the picture. "Fifty-one!" she exclaims.

155 Later, after Mr. Smith has caught the venomous spider on a glue trap, Ashanti tells me that there's an interesting-looking web woven through my trampoline's net.

"I spotted it today on one of my safaris," she says, grinning. "I want to photograph it."

"Stop by tomorrow, if you want," I say.

160 "It'll be early in the morning. That's the best time."

"I'll probably be awake."

"Just don't be bouncing, OK? You might wreck it."

"I don't want to do that," I say. "I want to know which spiders live in *my* yard."

165 Boy, won't Billy be surprised. I'll be able to teach him a thing or two about spiders when he comes to visit!

glances:

⑧ Reread and Discuss Reread lines 150–166. Discuss how Luis's opinions about spiders and about Ashanti have changed. Do you think they will be friends? Cite evidence from the text in your discussion.

SHORT RESPONSE

Cite Text Evidence What are some of Ashanti's characteristics? Cite details from the text in your response.

_____

_____

_____

_____

Background Did you know that the fire salamander shown below lives in Hungary? Do you have any idea what a newt looks like? It's the little reddish creature you see on page 131. This text introduces you to many amazing amphibians and to the sad fact that some of them are disappearing from this world. It also suggests ways to help them.

Setting a Purpose Read the text to learn about the amazing life cycles of amphibians and how you can help these creatures survive.

Amphibian Alert!

Informational Text by Elliott Meiner

① Read As you read, collect and cite text evidence.

- Underline text that explains what *amphibian* means.
- Circle details about the bodies of amphibians at different stages of their lives.

Frogs, toads, salamanders, and newts are amphibians. The word *amphibian* means "double life" because these animals live part of their lives in water and part of their lives on land. An

5 amphibian starts life in the water and then lives on land as an adult.

Amphibians lay their eggs in the water. These eggs do not have a hard shell. They are more like jelly. Young amphibians that hatch from the eggs

10 look very different from adult amphibians. The

young breathe with gills. They have tails that help them swim.

As young amphibians grow, their bodies change. They grow legs. Lungs develop and their gills disappear. These
15 changes allow amphibians to live on land and breathe air with their lungs.

The skin of amphibians is not protected by hair, feathers, or **scales** like other animals. Their skin is permeable, which means they can absorb air and water through their skin.

scales:

20 Amphibians are found on all the continents except Antarctica. They are ancient animals that have been around for about 360 million years. However, their lives are being seriously **threatened** in today's world.

threatened:

Scientists know of approximately 6,000 different kinds
25 of amphibians, but this number could change quickly. Scientists say that more than 120 amphibian species have already disappeared from the world. These kinds of amphibians are extinct, meaning that all members of the species have died.

30 Many different things are threatening the lives of amphibians, including **habitat** loss, pollution, introduced species, and a parasitic fungus. Scientists say that 2,000 to 3,000 of the amphibian species in the world are now threatened with extinction. It is the biggest extinction crisis
35 in today's world.

habitat:

2 Reread Reread lines 1–35. Why might amphibian species be especially threatened by extinction? Cite evidence from the text to support your answer.

_____

_____

_____

③ **Read** As you read, collect and cite text evidence.

- Underline the reasons amphibians need clean water.
- Circle the paragraph that explains how some ponds and creeks get polluted.
- Underline text that explains problems caused by the African clawed frog.

Habitat Loss and Pollution

Amphibians often live in swamps and ponds. But many of these swamps and ponds are being filled in to make way for roads, houses, and malls. Amphibians also live in rain forests that are being cut down or destroyed by
40 fire. The loss of these habitats often leaves the amphibians nowhere to live.

Clean water is extremely important to amphibians. Adult amphibians need clean water to keep their skin **moist.** Adults lay their eggs in water, and young
45 amphibians live completely in water.

Some ponds and creeks are close to farms. Chemical **fertilizers** are used on farms to grow better crops. Pesticides are used to kill insects that destroy crops. However, when it rains, these chemicals are washed into
50 the nearby ponds and creeks that lead to swamps and rivers.

Many frogs in these areas have been found with deformities, such as missing legs or extra legs. Deformed frogs like these have been found in 44 of the 50 United
55 States. Some scientists believe that the chemical pollution in the water is **absorbed** by the soft eggs of amphibians and by their permeable skin. The chemical pollution affects the eggs and growth of the young, causing these deformities.

moist:

fertilizers:

absorbed:

Introduced Species and Fungus

60 Since the 1930s African clawed frogs have been shipped around the world by the thousands. These frogs are used in laboratory studies and for other purposes. Some **exotic** amphibians are shipped to other countries as pets or for food. Sometimes these amphibians escape or are released

65 into their new habitat. In their new habitat they can cause problems.

exotic:

The introduction of African clawed frogs into new areas has caused two major problems. African clawed frogs are more aggressive than many frogs, and they have been

70 known to eat other frogs. But the bigger problem is that African clawed frogs carry a **fungus** called amphibian chytrid (KIT rid). This fungus does not hurt African clawed frogs, but it is deadly to many other kinds of amphibians.

fungus:

Scientists discovered this fungus in 1993. In the wild the

75 fungus is unstoppable and untreatable. It can kill 80 percent of the amphibians in an area within months. Scientists suspect that dozens of frog species have

80 gone extinct because of this fungus.

Most newts (like this one) and salamanders are found in the cool forests of North America, Europe, and northern Asia.

4 Reread Reread lines 60–81. What is an "introduced species," and how can it be dangerous to other species? Cite evidence from the text to support your answer.

_____

_____

_____

_____

⑤ Read As you read, collect and cite text evidence.

- Underline what scientists and conservation groups are doing to help save amphibians.
- Circle what you can do to help save amphibians.

Plans to Help

Scientists and **conservation** groups from around the world are putting plans together to help save amphibians. Much of their work focuses on the
85 amphibian chytrid fungus because the disease it causes is the most serious and immediate threat.

Some scientists are researching how the disease spreads and why
90 it kills only some individuals in one species, but kills all of another species. Other scientists are **assessing**
95 the damage the disease has caused. The areas most affected so far 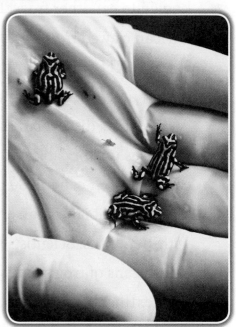 include Central America, the Caribbean, Australia, and parts of Asia. However, scientists warn there is no
100 continent or amphibian species that is safe.

Conservation groups that include many zoos are taking in many of the threatened amphibian species to protect and preserve them. In the future when the research scientists find ways to control the disease, the
105 conservation groups will release these animals back into their natural habitat.

conservation:

About 130 critically endangered Corroboree frogs (pictured at right) are being protected and preserved at Taronga Zoo in Sydney, Australia. Only about 200 of these frogs are left in the wild.

assessing:

What We Can Do

Like scientists, you can do research and learn as much as you can about the problems facing frogs and other amphibians. You can search the Internet using search

110 words, such as *threats to frogs and amphibians,* for more information. You can find maps and lists of the amphibian species in your area.

Amphibians live all over North America and in every state of the United States. The Appalachian range is home

115 to many different species. Contact local nature preserves, zoos, or the office of environmental matters in your state to learn about volunteer opportunities.

You can also help by keeping local ponds and creeks clean. Although these small habitats may not seem as

120 important as others, they are home to many creatures. We need to help preserve a future for them as well as for us.

⑥ Reread and Discuss Reread the ways you can help in lines 107–121. Discuss how you might go about doing these things. Then share which activities you think you might like to do and why.

SHORT RESPONSE

Cite Text Evidence How are scientists' efforts to help save amphibians different from those of conservationists? Use text evidence to support your response.

_____

_____

_____

_____

_____

Background There are art museums, science museums, historical museums, and nature museums. There are museums that focus on a single subject, like music boxes or postage stamps, and there are museums that seem to go in dozens of different directions at once. This text takes you on a tour of five very different ones.

Setting a Purpose Read the text to discover the kinds of collections and experiences five museums offer.

Museums
Worlds of Wonder

Informational Text by Jody Cosson

① Read As you read, collect and cite text evidence.

- Circle details about the City Museum's past and its mission.
- Underline details that show recycling is important to the museum.

Museums are wonderful places.

That doesn't just mean "terrific places." It means places that fill you with wonder—that surprise and amaze you. It also means places that
5   *make* you wonder—about the world, about nature, about history, about people.

Here is a brief tour of five museums that are very different from each other. But all of them are full of wonders.

City Museum

St. Louis, Missouri

10 The first thing you should know about the City Museum of St. Louis is that it is located in an old shoe factory. It's no surprise, then, that this museum believes in preserving the past and recycling—making something new out of something old. There's also an amazing playground called

15 MonstroCity that's made mostly of recycled materials from the city of St. Louis, including giant metal springs, a castle turret, and the body of a jet plane.

Artist Bob Cassilly designed the City Museum as a huge work of art. Take the Enchanted Caves. Where shoes once

20 moved on **conveyor belts** through tunnels, children now run into petrified dragons and climb spiral staircases. In Art City, you can watch glass blowers at work, and make your own work of art, too. Then there's the museum *inside* the museum. It's called The Museum of **Mirth,** Mystery,

25 and **Mayhem** and it's like an old-fashioned carnival. Finally, let's not forget the World Aquarium, home to more than 10,000 sea creatures, from stingrays to seahorses.

conveyor belts:

mirth:

mayhem:

(2) **Reread** Reread lines 10–27. Does the City Museum sound like a place you would like to visit? Explain why and cite evidence from the text to support your answer.

_____

_____

_____

_____

③ Read As you read, collect and cite text evidence.

- Underline the names of exhibits at the National Air and Space Museum.
- Circle some of the reasons you would want to visit Sue at the Field Museum.

National Air and Space Museum
Washington, DC

Are you interested in space and flight? Have you ever wondered where the Wright Brothers' original airplane
30 is? If so, then the National Air and Space Museum is the place for you. It has the largest collection of aircraft and spacecraft in the world.

milestones:

Begin with the **Milestones** of Flight Exhibit. You'll see the *Spirit of St. Louis,* the first plane to be flown
35 nonstop across the Atlantic Ocean by a solo pilot. Want some faster fliers? Check out the *Airacomet,* the first American jet, and the X-15, which flew six times the speed of sound! Upstairs you'll find the airplane that made it all possible: the *Flyer,* which Orville and Wilbur
40 Wright first flew in 1903.

Next, let your imagination soar into space. This

satellite:

museum is home to *Sputnik I,* the first **satellite** to successfully orbit Earth, and the *Apollo 11* command module, which carried the first men to the moon. Here
45 also are replicas of spacecraft that have flown to Mars, Venus, and Jupiter.

The Albert Einstein Planetarium lets you feel what it might be like to zoom through the galaxy. The Ride Simulator takes you on a virtual space walk. Finally,
50 there is a real moon rock you can touch that the *Apollo 17* astronauts brought back.

Field Museum

Chicago, Illinois

You could spend days exploring the Field Museum in the city of Chicago. The museum contains more than twenty million items, including **mummies, meteorites,** and

55 mammals. With so much to see, you might not have time to meet Sue. That would be a mistake.

Sue is the largest *Tyrannosaurus rex* skeleton ever found, as well as the most complete. Sue is forty-two feet long with more than two hundred bones—real bones, not plaster

60 ones. All except for Sue's second skull. It's a case of two heads being better than one.

Sue's five-foot-long skull was so big and heavy that the museum staff had to put it in a glass case by itself. They made a lighter model for the skeleton on display. You can

65 put your nose just inches from Sue's real skull—if you dare. You also can handle models of some of Sue's bones, including a huge tooth and a rib. By the way, Sue was named after Sue Hendrickson, the woman who found "her" in South Dakota. No one really knows if Sue is male

70 or female.

mummies:

meteorites:

④ Reread and Discuss Reread lines 52–70 and study the photo. Then discuss which impresses you more: the photo or the text. Give reasons and evidence to support your opinion.

⑤ **Read** As you read, collect and cite text evidence.

- Underline what you can learn about trees at the Discovery Museum.
- Circle what you can learn about cowboys at the American Cowboy Museum.

World Forestry Center and Discovery Museum

Portland, Oregon

A museum that's about trees? The World Forestry Center's Discovery Museum will make you appreciate forests more than ever before—including forests around the world.

75   On the first floor of the museum, you can explore forests that grow in the Pacific Northwest. You can discover what lives under the forest and then take a ride to explore the treetops. On another ride you can learn how smokejumpers fight forest fires. The museum shows

80   the many things that forests provide, such as wood, water, habitat, and clean air.

On the second floor, a giant wall map tells about different types of forests worldwide. Then you can see for yourself. Take a train ride to the forests of Siberia and

85   a boat ride to a forest lake in China. Ride a jeep to visit forest animals in South Africa. Look down on the **canopy** of Brazil's Amazon rainforest.

canopy:

138

American Cowboy Museum

Taylor-Stevenson Ranch near Houston, Texas

Many museums are important for changing old ideas
people may have. Through hands-on exhibits, talks, and
90 even horseback riding, the American Cowboy Museum
gives the true history of a popular legend. There is a lot we
can learn about the American cowboy. For example, did you
know that as many as one-third of all cowboys were African
Americans? Many cowboys were Native Americans, and the
95 first cowboys, or *vaqueros,* were from Mexico. And of
course, "cowboys" also included women.

The museum is part of the Taylor-Stevenson Ranch,
which is 150 years old. It has been owned by **generations** of
an African American family. About fifty years ago, the family
100 started the museum to honor the part Native Americans,
African Americans, Hispanics, and women played in settling
the West. The founders, Mollie Stevenson, Jr., and her mother,
Mollie Stevenson, Sr., are also the first living African
Americans in the National Cowgirl Hall of Fame.

generations:

6 Reread and Discuss Reread lines 71–104. Discuss which of these two
museums you would most like to visit, and why. Support your opinions with details
from the text.

SHORT RESPONSE

Cite Text Evidence What incorrect idea about cowboys might the founders of the
American Cowboy Museum be trying to change? How are they doing that? Use
text evidence to support your response.

_____

_____

_____

_____

Background When you are asked to speak or write about current events, do you think only about national events or do you also consider local ones? This readers' theater shows how four students research a local topic that matters to them and then work to change what is happening in their community.

Setting a Purpose Read the text to learn why the students want to save Timber Woods.

Save Timber Woods!

Readers' Theater by Lillian Dietrich

CLOSE READ
Notes

① **Read** As you read, collect and cite text evidence.
- Underline the stage directions that show what Gina does and feels.
- Circle the reason why Gina behaves this way.

Cast of Characters

Narrator

Lucas

Laura

Gina

Hector

Scene I

Setting: The kitchen in Gina's home on the edge of the woods

Narrator: Laura, Gina, Hector, and Lucas are researching a **current event** for school. Gina is searching on a laptop. The others are looking through newspapers.

Lucas: What if we do our report on gas prices?

5 **Laura:** Boring!

(Suddenly, Gina sees a deer outside in the yard. She jumps up from her chair and dashes to the kitchen door, shouting.)

Gina: Get out of there! Scram!

(Grabbing a broom, Gina charges out the door, waving the
10 *broom and yelling as the deer runs away.)*

Laura: Why did you yell at that deer, Gina? It was so cute.

Gina: *(Outraged)* Cute? Maybe, if you only see them once in a while; but they've started to show up in our yard every day. They are eating the tree we planted when my little
15 sister was born!

Narrator: Gina points at a small tree on the lawn. Its branches are nearly bare.

Gina: *(Calming down)* Those deer and our neighborhood don't go together.

CLOSE READ
Notes

current event:

---

2 Reread Reread lines 1–19. Based on Gina's actions, feelings, and statements, what might you conclude about her? Cite evidence from the text to support your answer.

_____

_____

_____

_____

_____

③ **Read** As you read, collect and cite text evidence.

- Underline dialogue that shows what characters value.
- Circle Gina's response to Hector's explanation for why deer are showing up in people's backyards.

20 **Hector:** We have deer at my house, too. My dad says it's because the deer have no place to go. People are building homes where the deer used to live. Now they have to find food somewhere else.

Gina: *(In an annoyed voice)* Well, not in my backyard.

25 **Lucas:** The poor deer lost their homes, Gina.

Gina: Well, my poor family is losing our favorite tree.

Hector: *(Holding up the newspaper he's been looking through, excitedly)* Hey! Listen to this! Here's an article that says the deer problem is going to get worse. Land

developers:

30 **developers** plan to cut down Timber Woods, by the school. Our town government has been renting the woods from a private owner. Now the owner plans to sell it to a developer who plans to build one hundred townhouses.

35 **Laura:** Timber Woods? That's where we do fieldwork for science class. That's where we camp and have picnics.

Lucas: What about the animals who live there? More animals will get kicked out of their homes.

Gina: More yards will be ruined by deer!

40 **Hector:** Well, at least we found a current event to report on.

Laura: I wish we could stop them from cutting down Timber Woods.

council:

Hector: Maybe it's not too late. The paper says that

45 people can talk about the development plan at next week's town **council** meeting. Let's ask our parents if we

can go. Right now, let's find more information to put into our current events report.

Gina: Let's get all the facts. That way we'll have a good
50 report for class and good ideas for the council meeting.

Lucas: Maybe our friends will come to the meeting.

Narrator: The group presents its current events report and the whole class gets excited. The class decides to ask the town's leaders to buy Timber Woods and preserve the land
55 for both animals and people.

Scene II

Setting: The next day, in the dining room of Gina's home

Narrator: The four friends are making signs for the meeting. Gina and Lucas are working on a large sign.

Laura: What is your sign going to say?

Gina and **Lucas:** "Save Timber Woods."
60 **Lucas:** "Save the animals from us . . . "

Gina: ". . . and save our yards from the animals!"

Hector: It's about the woods, too. Remember that book we read about the water cycle? It said that natural areas, such as woods, help absorb water and prevent flooding when heavy
65 rains fall or snow melts. But how can I put that on a sign?

Laura: How about: "Woods and water—important partners. Ask me why."

Hector: Good idea! Then I can talk about it when I give our statement.

CLOSE READ
Notes

4 Reread Reread lines 20–69. Which characters care more about the woods and animals than about their backyards? Cite text evidence to support your answer.

_____

_____

_____

⑤ **Read** As you read, collect and cite text evidence.

- Circle the key point Lucas realizes and how Hector thinks they should respond to it.
- Underline the clues that show Hector speaks well at the town council meeting.

70 **Gina:** It's cool that the town council said you could present a statement from us, Hector. But how will the town ever get enough money to buy the woods? I also heard my mom talking about how much money the city will get from new taxpayers who move into the new
75 houses.

Lucas: But the problems caused by cutting the woods will cost money. We have to help them see that.

Hector: *(Pointing at Lucas)* You're right. Instead of **ignoring** the issue of money, we should show that we
80 understand it. Let's do some more research so we know the facts. And how about this for a sign: "Saving Timber Woods saves dollars and makes sense."

Laura: At least the town will know how we feel.

ignoring:

Scene III

Setting: A meeting room with rows of folding chairs, inside the town hall

Hector: I'm nervous.

85 **Laura:** You're going to be great, Hector. Look, I think that's the developer!

Hector: Maybe he could tear down those old Smithfield **warehouses** and build homes there. Nobody has used those buildings for a long time.

90 **Lucas:** Good idea. *(Turning around)* I think the meeting's about to start.

warehouses:

Narrator: The town council members soon introduce the main topic: the sale of Timber Woods. People take turns talking about the plan to build townhouses. Finally, it's

95 Hector's turn to speak. The audience listens closely as he explains why the woods are so important, and what the students want the council to do.

Hector: (*In a firm voice*) So, we ask the adults in town to join us in finding a way to turn Timber Woods into

100 protected parkland. (*He sits down as many people applaud.*)

Narrator: After more debate, the council decides to delay the sale of Timber Woods for three months. During that time, the town will try to raise enough money to buy the woods. After the meeting, the students get together.

105 **Gina:** (*In an excited voice*) They listened to us after all.

Laura: Now we have to help find ways to raise money.

Lucas: How about a bake sale?

Hector: That's a good idea, but we'll need to do more than that.

110 **Laura:** Let's meet tomorrow.

Gina: Let's involve the whole class. Everyone will benefit if we can save Timber Woods, so we should all work together.

---

6 Reread and Discuss Reread lines 84–112. What ideas do the students come up with to help save the woods? Discuss the pros and cons of each idea.

SHORT RESPONSE

Cite Text Evidence Analyze Hector's character. What is he like? Cite evidence from the text to support your analysis.

_____

_____

_____

_____

Background What do mysteries have that other stories don't? A crime, clues, and someone who is suspected of the crime. In this mystery, you'll read about a group of kids who discover a few changes at a local pond. After following the clues and doing some research, they solve the mystery.

Setting a Purpose Read the text to follow the clues and solve the mystery of the strange new turtles that appear at Reed's Pond.

MYSTERY at Reed's Pond

Mystery by Zoe Zolbrod

CLOSE READ
Notes

① Read As you read, collect and cite text evidence.

- Circle the main characters in the story.
- Underline text that describes the story's setting.
- Circle the changes that the students notice at Reed's Pond.

assigned:

Once a week, Ms. Cabrera's science class spent an afternoon outside, working in teams to observe different habitats. Adrian, Mara, and Nicole were **assigned** pond patrol. Adrian wondered if his
5   team had gotten the best assignment because of his extra-sharp eyes.

Reed's Pond lay at the end of a shady, sloping path. Pine trees towered overhead. Bushes and moss-covered rocks rimmed the shore. Adrian had been the first one in class to
10 spot the turtle at the pond—even though its brown shell and wrinkled skin blended in perfectly with its surroundings.

"Here, Brownie . . . here, Brownie," Adrian whispered as he approached the water's edge. But today, the turtle that
15 peeked from the water looked different. Instead of a little brown face, this one had streaks of red near each eye.

"Brownie? Are you wearing makeup?" From what Adrian could see, the turtle's shell looked different, too. Today it was green with yellow stripes.

20 The girls hurried over. When the turtle came up for another breath, Nicole noticed the changes, too.

"That's not Brownie. That's a different kind of turtle," she said. "Its name should be Red Dot."

"Maybe Brownie's somewhere else," said Mara.

25 They continued their pond patrol, but Adrian had a strange feeling that something wasn't right. Sure enough, his hunch was correct.

"Look!" Mara shouted. She was pointing at a bird's nest or what used to be a bird's nest.

2 Reread Reread lines 13–29. Summarize the changes that Adrian, Mara, and Nicole discover at Reed's Pond.

_____

_____

_____

_____

(3) **Read** As you read, collect and cite text evidence.

- Underline the clue Mara finds and the questions the characters ask as they try to solve the mystery.
- Circle what the boy puts into the pond.

30   Just last week they had written about the nest in their logs. It was a carefully made cup of sticks nestled in a low-hanging branch. There had been three brown eggs in it. Now the branch was broken. The bowl was squashed into a messy ball.

35   "Where are the eggs?" asked Nicole.

    Adrian crouched under the branch, which jutted out over some rocks at the water's edge. He saw one egg smashed into a **crevice** between two rocks. He couldn't see any sign of the other two eggs.

40   "Do you think an animal did this to the nest?" Nicole wondered.

    "An animal couldn't have turned Brownie into Red Dot," said Adrian.

    "And an animal wouldn't have left this," said Mara.
45 She held up a shopping bag that she had found. "There's lettuce in it. Maybe it's a clue."

    "A clue to what?" asked Nicole.

    Ms. Cabrera's whistle blew. It was time to go back to class. "We need to do some more investigating," said
50 Mara. "Let's meet here Saturday, when we have more time."

    The weather on Saturday was sunny and warm, but no one else was at the pond. Nicole, Mara, and Adrian scanned the area. Adrian soon found the new turtle. It
55 sat **basking** on a rock at the edge of the water. When it saw the three children, it quickly slid into the water. The

crevice:

basking:

© Houghton Mifflin Harcourt Publishing Company

ripples spread and soon faded. Then Adrian, Mara, and
Nicole went to investigate the bird's nest. The clump of
sticks remained, but there were no new clues about what
60 had destroyed the nest or where the two eggs had gone.

ripples:

"This is the case of the missing turtle and eggs," Mara
said.

"Shh," whispered Adrian. He could hear leaves
crunching on the path. "Someone's coming. Hide!"

65 The three crouched in the bushes. Through the leaves,
they could see a teenaged boy wearing a blue backpack. At
the edge of the pond, the boy swung it from his shoulder
and knelt down. Adrian held his breath. He could hear his
heart beating. Had the boy noticed them?

70 The boy seemed to think he was alone, however. He
reached into his backpack and pulled out a turtle whose
shell was as big as a plate. It was bright green, with yellow
and green markings on the belly. Suddenly the turtle's head
shot out of the shell and snapped at the boy's wrist. The boy
75 dropped the turtle into the pond. The splash rang out as
loud as a slap. Adrian saw the red dashes on the turtle's face.

The boy **darted** back up the path and quickly vanished.

darted:

"So that's where Red Dot came from," whispered Nicole.

"Red Dot was already here on Thursday, though," said
80 Adrian. "This is the same kind of turtle, but it's not the
same turtle. Also, what about Brownie? Where's he?"

"We've got to talk to that boy," said Mara. "Come on."
Adrian wasn't sure it was a good idea, but Mara was already
running up the path. He and Nicole followed.

4 Reread and Discuss Reread lines 57–84. Discuss the mysteries. What do
you think happened to the brown turtle and the bird's nest? And why did the boy
leave the turtle? Cite evidence from the text in your discussion.

5 **Read** As you read, collect and cite text evidence.

- Circle facts that the students learn from their research.
- Underline text that describes what the officer does about the turtles.

striding:

85   "Excuse me!" Mara called out when she reached the field. The boy turned to look but kept **striding** toward his bike. "I just want to ask you about the turtle," Mara said.

    "I don't know what you're talking about," the boy

90 said. "I don't know anything about turtles." He got on his bike.

    "We just saw you drop one into the pond!" Mara shouted. It didn't matter. The boy pedaled off without looking back.

95   "Something fishy is going on," Nicole said.

    "Something turtle-y, you mean," replied Adrian.

    "I think it's time for a little research," said Mara.

    On Monday, they told Ms. Cabrera what they had seen. During science, she gave them time to research on

100 the computer. Mara typed the words *red dot turtle* into

search engine:

the **search engine.** Links for turtleneck sweaters, Turtle Island, and a video game came up.

    "This won't help," said Nicole.

    "Don't give up yet," said Mara. She typed in *red*

105 *turtle.* That was better. Lots of listings appeared for a turtle called a red-eared slider. The first thing Mara did was to click on the images.

    "That's it!" said Adrian, as a photo appeared. "That's Red Dot, all right."

110   With a few more mouse-clicks, the students learned that the turtles were common pets. They also learned

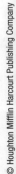

that the red-eared slider's natural habitat was east of the Rocky Mountains. "So what is one doing in a pond in California?" asked Nicole.

115   Mara typed *red-eared slider in California* into the search engine.

Among the listings of turtles for sale and questions about pet turtles, they saw an article from a California paper. The three of them read silently.

120   The article told about people dumping their pet turtles into local waters and the problems that occurred as a result. "Mystery solved!" said Mara.

"Ms. Cabrera!" they called.

"It looks like the pond patrol might have uncovered

125   some illegal activity," Ms. Cabrera said when they told her what they had learned. "Let's report it to the water **district**."

district:

That Thursday, Ms. Cabrera's class had a special observation day at the pond. Mr. Roberts, an officer from the water district, was with them. He had brought nets for

130   capturing the red-eared sliders. Adrian spotted the first one, basking near the ruined bird's nest. Working together, the class helped Mr. Roberts catch two more.

"We'll take them to a turtle sanctuary," Mr. Roberts explained. "It's a place where they keep the turtles safe until

135   someone can adopt them."

6 **Reread** Reread lines 110–126. How is the mystery solved? Cite evidence from the text in your answer.

_____

_____

_____

_____

151

(7) Read As you read, collect and cite text evidence.

- Underline details about each kind of turtle.
- Circle text that explains what might have happened to the bird's nest.

While Mr. Roberts talked, Adrian was looking for his old friend.

"Brownie!" said Adrian when he saw the head peek up. "Look, Mr. Roberts. That's the turtle I'm used to

140 seeing."

"That's a western pond turtle. It's just the kind of turtle we want to see around here."

"I never knew what kind he was. I just knew I liked him," said Adrian. *Western pond turtle*, he wrote in his

145 log.

"We got the sliders out just in time. Red-eared sliders are big. They eat the same things as the western pond turtles, and the western pond turtles can't compete," said Mr. Roberts.

150 "What about the bird eggs?" asked Nicole. "Did the turtles have anything to do with those?"

"Probably, but we can't be sure," said Mr. Roberts. "Red-eared sliders like to bask on nests. They can squash the nests and crush the eggs."

155 "That's another reason why people shouldn't leave their pets here," said Ms. Cabrera. She was posting a sign on a tree. DON'T DUMP YOUR PETS. BRING PET TURTLES TO VALLEY TURTLE SANCTUARY.

native: "Thanks for helping us save the **native** species," Mr.

160 Roberts told the class. "I have something for Adrian, Mara, and Nicole." He handed them each an envelope

and a patch that said *Water District* with a picture of a river.

165 "The water district invites you to be its first junior officers," Mr. Roberts said. "We'd also like to offer each of you a scholarship to **ecology** camp this summer. You can talk it over with your parents."

"Thanks!" said Adrian. He'd never thought his sharp eyes would actually help wildlife survive.

ecology:

⑧ **Reread and Discuss** Reread lines 146–158. Discuss the problem with dumping pets. Why might people do it? How does it affect the environment? Cite evidence from the text in your discussion.

SHORT RESPONSE

Cite Text Evidence   Mr. Roberts says they got the red-eared sliders out "just in time." What does he mean? What might have happened if they hadn't gotten the sliders out? Cite text evidence in your response.

_____

_____

_____

_____

Acknowledgments

"Dreams" from *The Collected Poems of Langston Hughes* by Langston Hughes, edited by Arnold Rampersad with David Roessel, Associate Editor. Text copyright © 1994 by The Estate of Langston Hughes. Reprinted by permission of Alfred A. Knopf, an imprint of the Knopf Doubleday Publishing Group, a division of Random House LLC, and Harold Ober Associates Incorporated. Any third party use of this material, outside of this publication, is prohibited. Interested parties must apply directly to Random House LLC for permission. All rights reserved.

"First Recorded 6,000-Year-Old Tree in America" from *A Burst of Firsts* by J. Patrick Lewis. Text copyright © 2001 by J. Patrick Lewis. Reprinted by permission of Curtis Brown, Ltd.

"The Song of the Night" by Leslie D. Perkins from *Song and Dance* selected by Lee Bennet Hopkins. Text copyright © 1997 by Leslie D. Perkins. Used by permission of Leslie D. Perkins, who controls all rights.